DUNKIRK AND THE LITTLE SHIPS

Philip Weir

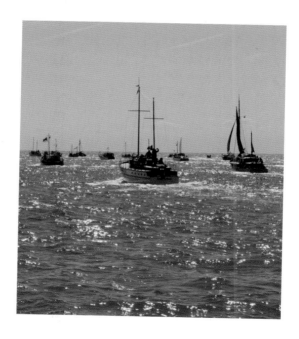

SHIRE PUBLICATIONS

Bloomsbury Publishing Plc

Kemp House, Chawley Park, Cumnor Hill, Oxford
OX2 9PH, UK

1385 Broadway, 5th Floor, New York, NY 10018,
USA

E-mail: shire@bloomsbury.com

www.shirebooks.co.uk

SHIRE is a trademark of Osprey Publishing Ltd

First published in Great Britain in 2020

A catalogue record for this book is available from the
British Library.

ISBN: PB 978 1 78442 375 9;
eBook 978 1 78442 376 6;
ePDF 978 1 78442 373 5;
XML 978 1 78442 374 2

20 21 22 23 24   10 9 8 7 6 5 4 3 2 1

Index by Zoe Ross

Typeset by PDQ Digital Media Solutions, Bungay, UK.

Printed and bound in India by Replika Press Private Ltd.

MIX
Paper from
responsible sources
FSC® C016779
www.fsc.org

Shire Publications supports the Woodland Trust, the
UK's leading woodland conservation charity.

COVER IMAGE

Front cover: A barge pulling a group of small boats
up the River Thames after their use in the Dunkirk
evacuation (Hulton-Deutsch/Corbis/Getty Images).
Back cover: A weathered commemorative plaque
on board one of the Dunkirk Little Ships (Peter
Macdiarmid/Getty Images).

TITLE PAGE IMAGE

Vessels of the Association of Dunkirk Little Ships
crossing the Channel.

CONTENTS PAGE IMAGE

The 30-foot naval pinnace MB *278* (with *Lazy Days*,
(unknown) and *Mada*).

ACKNOWLEDGEMENTS

Alamy, page 35; Andrew Curtis/CC BY SA 2.0, page 41;
Andrzej Otrębski/CC BY SA 4.0, page 103 (top); Ashley
Dace/CC BY SA 2.0, page 65 (bottom); Billy McCrorie/
CC BY SA 2.0, page 107;; Chris Allen/CC BY SA 2.0,
page 66 (top); Christine Matthews/CC BY SA 2.0, page
13 (bottom); daisybush/CC BY 2.0, page 87 (bottom);
Danny P Robinson/CC BY SA 2.0, page 103 (bottom);
David Hawgood/CC BY SA 2.0, page 68 (top); DerHexer/GNU, page 50; Elliott Simpson/CC BY SA
2.0, page 102 (top); Getty Images, pages 5, 9, 10, 11, 13
(top), 15, 20, 24, 26, 27, 28, 29 (bottom), 30, 32, 33,
37, 48, 51, 57, 58–9, 61, 69 (bottom), 70, 80 (both),
81, 82 (both), 83 (both), 85, 86, 87 (top), 88, 90 (both),
91, 93, 98; 100Hispalois/CC BY SA 4.0, page 22; Ian
Taylor/CC BY SA 2.0, page 21 (bottom); Jean Etienne
Minh Duy Poirrier/CC BY SA 2.0, page 40; John C.
Watkins/Public Domain, page 7; John Sutton/CC BY
SA 2.0, page 64; Jon Winfield/CC BY SA 2.0, page 65
(top); Lisa Jarvis/CC BY SA 2.0, page 102 (bottom); Lisa
Marie Turner, pages 42, 45, 46, 55 (both); Mark Longair/
CC BY SA 2.0, page 56; Nauda68/CC BY SA 4.0,
page 54; Nigel Sharp, pages 1, 3, 62–3, 66 (bottom), 67
(bottom), 68 (bottom), 69 (top), 71 (top), 71 (bottom),
72 (top), 73, 74 (top), 74 (bottom), 75 (top), 76–7, 101,
106 (bottom), 108, 109; Paul Reed, pages 21 (top), 23,
29 (top), 104, 106 (top); Peter Pearson/CC BY SA 2.0,
page 67 (top); Peter Turvey/CC BY ND 2.0, page 75
(bottom); Reading Tom/CC BY 2.0, pages 47, 89;
Richard Dorrell/CC BY SA 2.0, page 43; Richard Hoare/
CC BY SA 2.0, page 105 (bottom); Robert Cutts/CC
BY SA 2.0, page 105 (top); Stavros1/CC BY 3.0, page
99; The Carlisle Kid/CC BY SA 2.0, page72 (bottom);
Tom Lee/CC BY ND 2.0, page 53.

CONTENTS

THE FALL OF FRANCE

Thursday 9 May 1940 was a moment of political crisis for Britain. The war that had begun the previous September was not going well. Hitherto, it had been a bit of a strange war for those in the West. Indeed, the term 'Phoney War' was already appearing in the press. Apart from a short-lived and short-ranged French offensive in the opening days that got just 5 miles into German territory, the war on land had gone relatively quiet once Poland fell to Germany and the Soviet Union on 6 October 1939. In the air, although Warsaw had suffered terribly from both bombs and artillery as the Germans had laid siege, the great, catastrophic aerial bombing assaults against cities and their civilian populations that had been predicted even from the earliest days of manned flight, by the likes of the famous science fiction writer H.G. Wells, had simply not materialised. Even Britain's Royal Air Force (RAF) – perhaps the most committed of any of the world's air forces to strategic bombing – had been dropping millions of propaganda leaflets, rather than bombs, on German cities, in what became known as the 'Confetti War'. Only at sea had there been much real action.

With just two modern battleships, four heavy and six light cruisers in service at the outbreak of war, Germany's Kriegsmarine was spectacularly outmatched at sea by the massed fleets of the Allies and particularly Britain's Royal Navy. 'The only thing the fleet can do is to prove that it can sink honourably,' declared its own commander-in-chief, Grand Admiral

Erich Raeder. Nonetheless, with no land border for the army to cross and an air force really only configured to support the army, the sea was the only place Germany could seriously hope to damage Britain, attacking the massed ranks of shipping that brought food and raw materials to its people and

transported its people and equipment to war. Commanded by Commodore Karl Dönitz, the Kriegsmarine's U-boats would be key to this, much as had been the case during the First World War. By March 1940, some 200 Allied civilian and naval vessels had been lost, including the British battleship HMS *Royal Oak* and aircraft carrier HMS *Courageous*. What would become known as the 'Battle of the Atlantic' was in full swing, though it was by no means entirely one-sided. Largely contained in the North Sea and British coastal waters by distance and Allied control of the entrances to the Atlantic, by April the Germans had lost no fewer than 23 of the 39 U-boats with which they had started the war. The heavy cruiser *Admiral Graf Spee* had also been sunk in the early phases of this incredible battle of attrition.

German army units crossing a river in the Ardennes on 13 May 1940, showcasing both its horse and motorised transport.

It was events in the north that had brought the country to crisis point, however. Allied prevarication over the Soviet invasion of Finland in November 1939 had already brought down the government of Britain's key ally, France, with Prime Minister Édouard Daladier replaced by a figure considered to have more fight, Finance Minister Paul Reynaud, on 20 March 1940. When Germany then invaded Norway in April, Allied defeats and the evacuation of nearly 12,000 Allied troops from Åndalsnes and Namsos by 3 May ensured the fate of Prime Minister Neville Chamberlain echoed that of his French counterpart – he was replaced by another figure considered to have more fight than his predecessor, First Lord of the Admiralty Winston Churchill.

Yet in the midst of this crisis, events across the Channel exploded. At 0345 the following morning, before Chamberlain could formally issue his resignation, thousands of engines roared into life along Germany's borders with France and Belgium. At his new headquarters at Münstereifel, Adolf Hitler assembled his staff and pointed in the direction of the sound of distant artillery fire. After months of planning and preparation, he announced simply, 'Gentlemen, the offensive against the western powers has just started.'

The brainchild primarily of Lieutenant General Erich von Manstein, the German invasion plan had three parts. Army Group C, commanded by Colonel General Wilhelm Ritter von Leeb, was to directly attack the great French defences of the Maginot Line, keeping French troops there occupied. Army Group B, under Colonel General Fedor von Bock, backed by the lion's share of the aircraft, was to invade the Netherlands and central Belgium, spearheaded by daring, airborne assaults from the Luftwaffe's Fallschirmjäger paratroops against a series of Dutch airfields, bridges, and even the Dutch high command and royal family, as well as fortifications, such as the key Belgian fortress at Eben-Emael. Meanwhile, Army Group A, under Colonel General Gerd von Rundstedt, with the most tanks and troops, would attack through Belgium and Luxembourg, entering France just 10 miles from the northern end of the famous Maginot Line. The aim was to split the Allied armies at a weak spot in the defences, through the difficult terrain of the Ardennes forest, reach and cross the Meuse River at Sedan, then push round behind them, on to the Channel coast, encircling the bulk of those armies and trapping them. It was an extremely high-risk manoeuvre. The German Army in mid-1940 had a spearhead of highly mechanised panzer divisions, but its far larger mass of infantry remained heavily reliant upon horses for transport. To successfully encircle the Allies' northern armies, von Rundstedt's panzers would therefore have to push on far faster than his infantry, leaving the panzers vulnerable to a swift counter-attack that could cut them off instead.

The entrance to Ouvrage Schoenenbourg in Alsace, France, one of the key fortifications of the Maginot Line, which bore the brunt of the final German assault on the line from 15 June, eventually surrendering after the armistice on 1 July 1940, and now open to the public as a museum.

A triumph of the military engineer's art, the Maginot Line was perhaps the most formidable and sophisticated defensive line in the world at the time, but famously, it did not extend down the Franco–Belgian border to the sea. To do so would have been both expensive and politically problematic, leaving neutral Belgium looking cut off and abandoned by one of its guarantors under the 1839 Treaty of London. Consequently, it was well known, even intended, that the Germans would be forced to go north. There, they would be met by the bulk of France's finest troops, ensuring that the next war would not be fought on French soil, avoiding a repeat of the grievous casualties and damage to towns and cities that had been suffered between 1914 and 1918. An added advantage for France was that any German invasion of neutral Belgium would almost certainly draw the similarly treaty-bound Britain into war once more.

In the event, the British arrived before the invasion of Belgium. A new British Expeditionary Force (BEF) had been formed the day war was declared, and placed under the command of no less a figure than the British Army's professional head, Chief of the Imperial General Staff and a Victoria Cross-winning hero of the First World War, General John Vereker, 6th Viscount Gort. The advanced parties sailed from Portsmouth aboard Royal Navy destroyers on 4 September, followed by the first big troop convoys, leaving Southampton and the Bristol Channel on the 9th. Protecting these convoys was an ageing, though still powerful, fleet – the Channel Force, made up of the battleships HMS *Resolution* and HMS *Revenge*, along with the aircraft carriers HMS *Courageous* and HMS *Hermes*, assembled at Portland and Plymouth under the command of rising naval star Rear Admiral Lancelot Holland.

Despite the massive British armies that had fought in continental Europe not only in the First World War but also in various wars before that, a similar such commitment was still in doubt. Britain had spent the inter-war years once more accepting only limited liability on the Continent. Only on 6 February 1939 had Chamberlain announced that an attack upon French interests would 'evoke the immediate co-operation of Great Britain'. This new BEF was therefore a relatively small force that would reach a peak strength of just ten infantry divisions and an armoured brigade. Nevertheless, it was the best the British Army had to offer, comprising most of its pre-war regulars and reserves. It was also highly mechanised and therefore highly mobile, with perhaps the highest proportion of vehicles to troops of any army in the world (to the point where, when it was discovered some animal transport would be useful, Cypriot and Indian units had to be drafted in). Attached for air support were 13 RAF squadrons – mostly Westland Lysander reconnaissance aircraft and Hawker Hurricanes for fighter protection – commanded by Air Vice Marshal Charles Blount. A further 12 squadrons of Bristol Blenheim and Fairey Battle bombers, with more Hawker Hurricane fighters, commanded by Air Vice Marshal Patrick Playfair, formed the independent Advanced Air Striking Force (AASF). The first squadrons of Playfair's AASF had been the first British force to arrive on French soil, flying into bases near Rheims the day before war was declared, just in case the new war should open with an immediate attack.

Key to the war plan developed by Supreme Commander of Allied Forces in France, French General Maurice Gamelin, was correctly deducing the German invasion route. Its importance only increased in March, when Gamelin, in a perhaps

uncharacteristic show of flair, adapted his plan to get General Henri Giraud's 7th Army, hitherto his mobile reserve that would have countered any German breakthrough, to push even further on through Belgium and try to join up with the Dutch at Breda, aiding that country, and safeguarding one of Europe's biggest ports at Antwerp. Fatally, however, the French had long considered the most likely German invasion route to be through the Gembloux Gap, across Belgium's central plain. An extraordinarily successful German campaign of deception and disinformation further cemented this in the minds of Gamelin and his staff. Even intelligence gained by breaking the famous Enigma communication codes of the Luftwaffe (with the assistance of the Poles) did not help, as this only further emphasised its concentration on Army Group B. Gamelin therefore made the Dyle River east of Brussels the key objective his forces needed to reach and defend, assigning General Gaston Billotte's First Army Group, made up of the Allies' best and most mobile mechanised formations, including the BEF, to the task. Consequently, when Billotte's forces began to cross the border at 0650 on 10 May, they soon passed, unknowingly, von Rundstedt's panzers. The panzers were, of course, heading in precisely the opposite direction, but just a few miles south, where, rather than meeting Gamelin's main force, they

Troops of the new British Expeditionary Force disembarking in France from the troopship SS *Worthing*, a 2,350-ton Southern Railway cross-Channel ferry. After spending the war as a troopship, hospital ship, and amphibious landing ship, *Worthing* resumed commercial service, being sold to Greece in 1954, then scrapped in 1968.

Luftwaffe Fallschirmjäger parachuting near the Meuse bridge at Moerdijk, Netherlands, 10 May 1940. The Fallschirmjäger's aim was to capture Dutch bridges, fortifications and even leaders 'to sever the head from the snake', as their leader, Lieutenant General Kurt Student, rather colourfully put it.

quickly smashed through the few light Belgian and French divisions that protected the Ardennes.

It is easy to criticise Gamelin's judgement, and not merely in hindsight. Indeed, it is not impossible to pinpoint his staking everything on the route through central Belgium as the decision that lost France the war. As is so often the case there were even warnings at the time, most notably from exercises conducted by General André-Gaston Prételat in 1938, that predicted a German armoured thrust through the Ardennes could reach Sedan in 60 hours. Yet it must also be said that Gamelin had made a logical deduction based upon a conventionally sound assessment of the terrain. The Gembloux Gap was a traditional invasion route that lacked significant natural barriers, such as the great rivers and forests of the Ardennes. The perils of these were amply demonstrated that first day by the creation of the world's biggest traffic jam of panzers and their support vehicles, snaking along the forest roads, a tempting target for Allied aircraft had they too not been occupied to the north. Indeed, the Gembloux Gap might well have actually been the German route had an aircraft containing Majors Helmuth Reinberger and Erich Hoenmanns not made a forced landing in Belgium on 10 January while carrying copies of the plans, forcing the Germans into a radical rethink. The French Army in May 1940 suffered from a multitude of problems – in leadership, in air support, in command and control, in mobility, in morale, in training, and of course counter-factual scenarios are impossible to prove, but some of its defensive performances in the aftermath of Dunkirk do raise questions about what might have happened had the two armies met head-to-head.

The German offensives met with some astonishing successes on that first day, though they were not without cost and did not always achieve their aim. Fierce Dutch resistance ensured that Student's daring airborne assaults proved especially costly. Some were pushed back, particularly around The Hague, while losses to their Junkers Ju 52 transport aircraft, partly from Dutch action, but mainly crash landings, made 10 May one of the Luftwaffe's costliest days. Greater success had been achieved around Rotterdam. The Dutch Navy's most modern, home-based destroyer, HNLMS *Van Galen*, had been sunk attempting to provide gunfire support to the defence of that city, while the Dutch air forces had taken a savage beating.

The home-based Dutch Army was just 280,000 strong and poorly organised and equipped, with few tanks or artillery pieces, while the Dutch air forces had just 70 modern aircraft. Like the Belgians, the Dutch relied on neutrality to protect them. If this failed the Netherlands

Major General Erwin Rommel's 7th Panzer Division, preparing to cross the River Meuse near Sedan, where French defences were weak.

had significant natural defences, particularly floodable areas known as the Waterline, behind which they hoped to hold out for up to three months before help arrived. In the event, the Admiralty ordered the cruiser HMS *Birmingham* and nine destroyers, already at sea off Denmark, to head for Terschelling at 0621 that morning to assist and, crucially, stop any German attempts to combine their airborne and conventional assaults with seaborne landings, as they had done in Denmark and Norway. Meanwhile, minesweepers sailed from Sheerness to deal with mines dropped by the Luftwaffe.

The Allies could now use Dutch ports and their naval superiority to quickly bring up reinforcements by sea, so while the first mechanised units of Giraud's 7th Army arrived at the Dutch border that evening, a number of ferries, escorted by the destroyers HMS *Valentine*, HMS *Winchester* and the French *Cyclone* and *Sirocco*, began landing the infantry at Vlissingen the following morning. Much to their distress, however, they found the Dutch already leaving. Due to fears of being outflanked, Dutch Commander-in-Chief, General Henri Winkelman had decided to abandon the area. Despite the French arrival, the Dutch did not return and the French advanced no further than the city of Tilburg, so the linkup of the two armies was never fully established.

Various Anglo–Dutch arrangements put in place the previous year were now enacted, under the command of Admiral Sir Reginald Drax, the Commander-in-Chief Nore, based at Chatham. On 11 May the cruisers HMS *Arethusa* and HMS *Galatea* escorted Dutch gold reserves out of Ijmuiden, while the surviving elements of the Royal Netherlands Navy, led by the cruiser HNLMS *Sumatra*, evacuated their bases heading for the Medway. The Koninklijke Marine was probably in the best shape of the Dutch armed services. A comparatively small force of cruisers and destroyers, much of which was stationed in the Dutch East Indies to protect against Japanese aggression when the German invasion began, it was technologically advanced, having received a substantial amount of Dutch rearmament spending, and had a number of vessels nearing completion with cutting-edge new systems. Key among them were the cruiser HNLMS *Jacob van Heemskerck* and destroyer HNLMS *Isaac Sweers*, with examples of the world-beating Hazemayer gyroscopically stabilised anti-aircraft fire control system. Similarly, the incomplete submarines *O-21*, *O-22*, *O-23* and *O-24*, with snorkel technology that allowed them to remain submerged while charging their batteries, were successfully either sailed or towed across to Britain by their crews to be completed and fight alongside the Royal Navy, their technological advances passed on to their new allies. Three of *Isaac Sweers'* sister ships, along with *O-25*, *O-26* and *O-27* (and notably their snorkel technology), were too incomplete to move, and so were captured by the Germans, who similarly completed and commissioned them all into the Kriegsmarine.

Admiral Sir Reginald Drax, whose responsibilities as Commander-in-Chief Nore stretched from Scotland to the English Channel.

Admiralty House, the Commander-in-Chief Nore's residence at Chatham. Below ground lies a network of tunnels, from which Drax commanded operations (now part of the University of Kent Medway campus).

On 12 May, 200 Royal Marines also landed ashore at Hook of Holland from the destroyers HMS *Venomous* and HMS *Verity*. They did not herald the arrival of the three British Army divisions Winkelman had hoped for, however. Instead they were securing the port for the landing of the 2nd Battalion, Irish Guards, who were simply there to evacuate the Dutch royal family and government, and British Embassy staff and citizens. British ground forces were just spread too thin to do more. The BEF, at that very moment racing into the heart of Belgium under French command, had first call on troops based at home. Many spare units had been sent to Norway where, in April, in a move reminiscent of previous wars, it had even been deemed necessary to scrape together a 600-strong naval brigade of sailors and marines from crews of ships in refit to get numbers to support an attack on the port of Trondheim. The increasing Italian threat meant withdrawing troops from the Middle East was also a non-starter, even if they could have arrived in time. Meanwhile the Royal Marines, who might have provided some more light infantry, had first been sent to occupy the Faroe Islands in April, then neutral Iceland in May, securing Allied control of the entrances to the Atlantic. Their main available force under Colonel Robert Sturges arrived at Reykjavik aboard the cruisers HMS *Berwick* and HMS *Glasgow* the day the panzers rolled west.

A reluctant Queen Wilhelmina and her government were evacuated on the 13th aboard HMS *Hereward* and HMS *Windsor*, leaving Winkelman as the highest remaining government authority. The following morning, the Marines and Guards were finally brought out aboard HMS *Malcolm*, HMS *Whitshed* and HMS *Vesper*, having demolished any harbour facilities they could to prevent their being of use to the Germans. As they left, the Germans were threatening to destroy Rotterdam. Controversially, the bombing raid actually took place during negotiations, causing serious damage and around

HMS *Windsor*, a 1,100-ton W Class destroyer commissioned in June 1918. Commanded by Lieutenant Commander Peter Pelly, *Windsor* evacuated the Dutch Government, then 3,991 men from Dunkirk, before spending the remainder of the war in the Arctic, Channel and North Sea.

850 deaths. Colonel Pierre Scharroo surrendered the city shortly afterwards. An hour later, Winkelman assembled his senior commanders. With other cities under similar threat, defensive lines crumbling and no prospect of further Allied help, he took the decision to surrender and avoid pointless bloodshed.

Not all the Dutch armed forces laid down their arms that evening. Some, who later proved of great use to the Allied war effort, managed to escape. Carrying their designs, the radar engineers Max Staal and J.L.W.C. von Weiler had already escaped that morning aboard the destroyer HMS *Wessex*, accompanied by the British naval attaché, Admiral Sir Gerald Dickens (grandson of the famous author Charles Dickens). The chief of the Dutch naval staff, Vice Admiral Johannes Furstner, also managed to escape that day, but by fishing boat, rather than Royal Navy destroyer. Similarly, Commander Jules Schagen van Leeuwen and the team behind the development of the Hazemayer fire control system made their own way past German lines, out of Den Helder and across to Britain, where they spent the rest of the war working for the Naval Ordnance Department.

The combined naval and military forces in the province of Zeeland, commanded by Rear Admiral Hendrik Jan van der Stad, fought on alongside the French. Here too, though, resistance was rapidly collapsing and the French quickly began evacuating their troops by land and sea. On the 15th, *Valentine*, this time with HMS *Whitley*, came under air attack while protecting those crossing the River Scheldt to Terneuzen. Australian commander Herbert Buchanan spectacularly ran his ship aground after taking a bomb hit that punched a massive hole in the bow. '[A] good stiff one as soon as we were ashore', courtesy of 'medical supplies' of whiskey and sherry, and Buchanan and his crew began their trek from Terneuzen towards France and safety. They were joined by thousands of French troops and a number of Dutch, some of whom cycled their way up the coast. Their collective destination was the French port of Dunkirk, where Buchanan and his men arrived on the 17th, the day van der Stad's forces effectively surrendered Zeeland.

If the news from the Netherlands on the 14th was dire for the Allies, the news from France was, if anything, worse, for on that day the defences at Sedan gave out, allowing von Rundstedt's panzers to begin crossing the River Meuse. Allied air forces now put everything into a desperate effort to halt the German advance. The bulk of the effort fell on to the Hurricanes, Battles and Blenheims of Playfair's AASF. The results were shattering. Of 109 RAF bombers that took off in various attacks that day, no fewer than 45 failed to return. The French lost another eight. Fifty fighters were shot down trying to protect them. The courage of the Allied pilots certainly made an impression upon their opponents; their bombs, however, did not, and panzers continued to pour across the Meuse. By now Billotte's armies, including the BEF, were battling Army Group B on the Dyle River, blunting its attacks, as had long been planned, but to no avail. The Allies had been comprehensively outflanked.

Army Group A was now in behind them and on their way to the Channel coast. The following day, Gamelin realised he had little choice but to order his forces in Belgium to begin a phased withdrawal to the River Scheldt, telling Daladier in a phone call that evening that he had no reserves left to make a counter-attack. 'Then the French Army is finished?' asked the Minister of War. 'It's finished,' replied the Supreme Commander.

It was at this point that the change of government — still just a few days old — coupled with the unfolding disaster on the Continent, prompted a decision to radically change the way Britain would fight the war. Needing to swiftly effect events on the Continent, but lacking a massive army with which to try to shore up its allies, the country would turn to its air power. Pressure from Gort, the commander of British Air Forces in France, Air Marshal Arthur Barratt, and particularly the French, to increase efforts in France, was intense. Yet on the 15th the War Cabinet took a rather different decision. Championed by the Lord Privy Seal, Clement Attlee, approval was granted for Air Marshal Charles Portal's RAF Bomber Command to commence a strategic bombing campaign against military, industrial and other targets in Germany, even if it resulted in civilian casualties.

Although not directly supporting the forces in France, it was hoped this new strategic bombing campaign would not only damage German industry, but also relieve some of the pressure at the front, firstly by forcing the Luftwaffe to divert fighters to home defence, and secondly by goading Germany into direct retaliation against Britain. This would take some bombers away from the front too, drawing them directly onto Britain's powerful, sophisticated, air defence system, which would have a better chance of shooting them down than the forces in France. However, this new strategy was incompatible with fresh promises by Churchill, personally to Reynaud, to send additional RAF fighter squadrons to France, prompting a famously stark warning letter from the commander-in-chief, RAF Fighter Command, later immortalised in the 1969 film *The Battle of Britain* by the voice of actor Sir Lawrence Olivier. 'If the Home Defence Force is drained away in desperate attempts to remedy the situation in France,' wrote Air Chief Marshal Sir Hugh Dowding, 'defeat in France will involve the final, complete and irremediable defeat of this country.' His appeal was successful and no more aircraft were sent across the Channel; the depleted squadrons that remained in France were instead temporarily combined, where possible, to make complete units.

The first major raid of Britain's new strategic bombing campaign took place the night after Rotterdam. The 99 big Handley Page Hampden, Vickers Wellington and Armstrong Whitworth Whitley bombers that took part were divided between various oil and rail targets scattered across the Ruhr valley, and thanks to desperately primitive navigation, just 24 of them claimed to have even seen, let alone hit, their targets. The Luftwaffe did end up diverting its efforts, but only in September when raids on Berlin and other cities famously played a part in the German decision to move from attacking Fighter Command to attacking London, halfway through the Battle of Britain. The gloves had been taken off, but British air power would not turn the tide, particularly not at that late hour, and certainly not with the level of capability it then possessed. It would be some time before Bomber Command could unleash the massive attacks on cities that had long been feared, and with which it would later become associated after Berlin, Hamburg and Dresden; seriously dislocating Germany's efforts in the air, and indeed the war in general, would take years to realise. Nonetheless, whatever its shortcomings in May 1940, strategic bombing was what Bomber Command had been created, equipped, and had long trained, planned and lobbied for. Its 'Confetti War' was now very much over.

THE EVACUATION

IN THE EARLY hours of 21 May, the lead elements of Army Group A's spearhead, the 2nd Panzer Division, sighted the coast west of Noyelles. Forty-five Allied divisions – Belgian, British and French – were now encircled, trapped in a pocket 120 miles long and 85 miles deep. Just two days before, Gamelin had ordered a counter-offensive by Billotte's First Army Group to try to cut through the vulnerable flanks of Army Group A's thrust to the coast, trapping them instead. That very evening, however, he was sacked by Reynaud (along with a number of others), to be replaced as Supreme Commander by France's Commander-in-Chief Orient, General Maxime Weygand, on 19 May. Weygand's first move was to cancel the counter-offensive.

With French command in chaos and knowing that his force was in severe danger of being cut off, on 18 May Gort had already ordered his staff to begin planning for the possibility that the BEF might have to be evacuated through the Channel ports. The following day, he informed London, and at a meeting in the War Office, Vice Admiral Bertram Ramsay, in charge of the Dover sector (previously part of Drax's Nore command), was placed in charge of any such operation. Returning to his headquarters at Dover Castle, Ramsay assembled his staff and began making arrangements. He had a number of destroyers and 30 or so passenger ships at his disposal to evacuate people from ports, but it was also recognised that some would need to be brought off beaches. Unfortunately, the gentle gradient

Admiral Sir Bertram Ramsay, a brilliant planner recalled from retirement to reconstitute the famous Dover command just days before the outbreak of war.

of the beaches in that part of France meant that the destroyers and other, bigger, ships would need to sit some distance offshore, with men being ferried out to them by small boats such as the ships' own lifeboats. This would be an extremely slow process, so to speed things up, Ramsay's staff began looking for other boats with shallow drafts that could be sent across the Channel to help with the ferrying. They initially alighted particularly upon around 50 Dutch barges, or 'schuyts', which had so recently been evacuated from their own country and were now assembled in the southern ports. Preparations began for them to be crewed by spare naval personnel and sent to France to help, but these alone would not be sufficient, and soon virtually nothing that floated in a southern naval base would be safe. Even Ramsay's personal admiral's barge would be dispatched across the Channel under the command of a young sub-lieutenant named Beale.

At the same time, Gort was authorising the evacuation of the first element of his command. With communications disrupted and airfields threatened, it was felt that the remnants of Blount's Air Component could assist more effectively from Britain. Ground crews would have to follow by land and sea, but the majority of the fighter and reconnaissance squadrons flew back across the Channel on the 20th. Blount himself was to set up his new headquarters at RAF Hawkinge. Permission was also granted to begin withdrawing other surplus, non-fighting men (some logistics troops, administrators, and others generally vital for running an army, but not absolutely necessary for the immediate defence of the area and organisation of an evacuation).

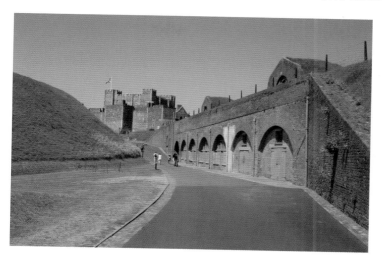

Dover Castle, home of the Flag Officer commanding Dover. It possesses a network of tunnels that contained Ramsay's headquarters. Unlike those at Chatham, these tunnels have been preserved and opened to the public as a museum by English Heritage.

The French were busy too, concerned that Dunkirk was flooded with refugees, both uniformed and civilian, and that the Germans were about to close off the land routes out. The French Army's commander in Dunkirk, Brigadier General Jules-Henri Watrin, and the commander of French naval forces in the north, Vice Admiral Jean-Marie Abrial – Ramsay's French opposite number headquartered in Dunkirk's Bastion 32 – organised a convoy to begin evacuating people who

Communications equipment in the preserved tunnels at Dover Castle. Much like Admiralty House at Chatham, Dover Castle possesses a network of tunnels from which Ramsay commanded the evacuation. The tunnels at Dover have been preserved and opened to the public as a museum by English Heritage.

Bastion 32, headquarters of Amiral Nord, Vice Admiral Jean-Marie Abrial, the commander of French naval forces in the north and Ramsay's French opposite number. Bastion 32 is now open to the public as a museum.

would not contribute to the defence, and material that was needed elsewhere. Among these were approximately 2,000 Dutch, nearly 1,500 of whom were loaded aboard the 4,000-ton, Glasgow-built, French freighter SS *Pavon* on the 20th. That evening they departed for Cherbourg, van der Stad wanting to take them away to reorganise, re-equip and reform as the core of a new Dutch legion.

What followed was an unpleasant foretaste of the perils to come for the Allies generally, and a disaster for the Dutch in particular. Having observed the loading of the ships, Junkers Ju 88 bombers of the Luftwaffe's Kampfgeschwader 30 attacked as the ships were leaving. The 13,921-ton tanker *Salome* failed even to make it out of the harbour before being seriously damaged, while the French destroyer *L'Adroit*, waiting outside as part of the escort, was struck by a bomb in the bow. Much as Buchanan had done in similar circumstances with HMS *Valentine*, Lieutenant Commander Henri Dupin de Saint-Cyr quickly put his ship aground on the beach at Malo-les-Baines, abandoning it before a spectacular explosion tore through the forward magazines. *Pavon* got a few miles before being hit, but the damage was fatal, and Captain Perdrault put his ship aground at Les Hemmes d'Oye. The Dutch used ropes to clamber down the *Pavon*'s hull and onto the beach. Fifty of their comrades would never leave, but the remainder assembled at the village of Coquelles, just west of Calais, where they would be taken prisoner by the advancing Germans on the 24th.

In an unfortunate coincidence, while driving south from Dunkirk, van der Stad's car suddenly found itself in the midst of a German column, losing the Dutch their commander-in-chief at almost the same time as his troops were abandoning the *Pavon*. Of perhaps more importance, however, was the collision with a refugee lorry that claimed the life of Billotte just hours later, further disrupting the French chain of command just as the British, with some French units, were attempting a small counter-attack of their own at Arras, and Weygand was planning a closely associated counter-offensive. Despite very limited tactical success on the ground, Gort's mini-offensive on 21 May did have one significant impact. It was enough to shake some members of the German high command into believing that the Allies might just be able to cut off and entrap the exposed spearhead of von Rundstedt's Army Group A that had just reached the Channel. As a result, even though the Weygand Plan never got off the ground, late on the 23rd, von Rundstedt's panzers were ordered to halt for

The wreck of the L'Adroit-Class destroyer *L'Adroit* at Malo-les-Bains. Commissioned in 1929 and lost just before the main evacuation began, the shattered hull of the 2,000-ton warship, lying on the beach, would become one of the iconic sights of the evacuation and its aftermath.

rest, repair and replenishment while the infantry caught up to protect the vulnerable flanks. They would not be permitted to resume for another three, vital, days.

Ports were now crucial for the Allies. In the best-case scenario, they were the only way of getting enough food, water, fuel, ammunition and reinforcements ashore to allow the armies to hold out. They were also the only way of conducting an evacuation quickly – getting men in large numbers directly from shore onto big ships and away. So while Gort's attack was spooking the Germans at Arras, the 20th Guards Brigade, including the 2nd Battalion, Irish Guards, who were now familiar with securing ports after their Dutch adventures, stepped ashore at Boulogne with a Royal Marine detachment. Despite the presence of the French 21st Infantry Division, RAF fighter protection and gunfire support from eight British and three French destroyers, their stay would be short and bloody. Surrounded and under heavy attack, the Guards were preparing to make their final stand on the afternoon of the 23rd when Ramsay was ordered to evacuate them and demolish the harbour. The destroyers quickly switched from gunfire support to transport, entering the harbour in pairs to successfully bring out 4,368 men. No ships were lost, though the danger to crews was illustrated when a sniper killed the operation's commander, Captain David Simpson, on the bridge of HMS *Keith* while the Guards were boarding. Five hundred men could not be extracted, surrendering along with the French 21st Division on 25 May.

30th Brigade, similarly delivered to Calais, would not be so fortunate.

An unknown hospital ship evacuating wounded troops of the 20th Guards Brigade from Boulogne, on or around 23 May 1940.

Attacked from three sides on the 24th, they had some success, but once more, despite the assistance of the RAF and a force of British and Polish destroyers, from which HMS *Wessex* was lost, the defences began faltering. Preparations to evacuate were interrupted by the arrival of Vice Admiral Sir James Somerville aboard HMS *Wolfhound*. Another recalled retiree at the Admiralty who was now assisting Ramsay at Dover, Somerville hand-delivered the devastating message that the French had ordered no evacuation could take place, and the 30th 'must comply for the sake of Allied solidarity'. Aided by additional firepower from the 6-inch guns of the modern cruisers HMS *Arethusa* and HMS *Galatea*, Brigadier General Claude Nicholson and his men held on for a further two, brutal days, finally succumbing on the afternoon of the 26th. Around 200 soldiers and Marines made it out that night aboard the naval yachts *Conidaw* and *Gulzar*. A note that morning from the chief of staff of the Belgian Army, Lieutenant General Oscar Michiels, warning of an impending Belgian collapse, had all but ruled out Ostend too. All that was left now, if the Allied armies were to evacuate, was Dunkirk.

The order that 'Operation *Dynamo* is to commence' was sent to Ramsay at 1857, just three hours after Nicholson surrendered. This was the signal for things to begin in earnest, and the first vessel – the 2,750-ton Manx packet SS *Mona's Queen* – sailed from the Downs at 2116, but in truth, a lot was already happening. After all, the Royal Navy's southern commands at the Nore, Dover, Portsmouth and Plymouth had been steadily receiving reinforcements since the German invasion, the Allied armies in the area had already fallen back into a defensive perimeter around Dunkirk, while around 23,000 of the BEF's surplus, non-fighting men had already evacuated since the 20th, and ships had been arriving throughout the day. Another Manx packet, the 1,600-ton SS *King Orry*, had been the first ship to sail from Britain on the 26th, leaving at 0930.

Little ships being towed back up the Thames on 9 June 1940, much as they had departed several days earlier. The 40-foot motor cruiser *Ryegate II* (rear) broke down at Dunkirk, but survived and is an active member of the Association of Dunkirk Little Ships.

Ramsay and his staff believed they now had two days, in which they calculated that with the ships and facilities they had, they could evacuate 45,000 men. It was not just a case of sailing the 51 miles straight from Dunkirk to the disembarkation ports at Dover, Folkestone, Margate and Ramsgate, either. There were three routes across the Channel from Dunkirk, imaginatively named 'X', 'Y' and 'Z'. The latter was the most direct route that took ships towards Calais, leaving them briefly under the guns of German artillery now on the coast that had already damaged *King Orry*, returning loaded with 1,131 troops. 'X' was the central route through the worst of the local sandbanks but was blocked by Allied minefields that would take the minesweepers HMS *Halcyon* and HMS *Skipjack* a couple of days of painstaking, dangerous work to clear. Route 'Y' was the northernmost, but also the longest route, taking ships out towards Antwerp, before doubling back on themselves and heading for Britain: a journey of 172 miles.

The following morning, another retired officer stepped in. Vice Admiral Sir Lionel Preston had been recalled at around the same time as Ramsay, initially to advise on minesweeping, but had been given command of the Small Boats Pool. By a remarkable stroke of luck, while the Allies were suffering the catastrophes of 14 May, the Admiralty had requested that the public register all self-propelled pleasure craft between 30 and 100 feet in length. Preston's team and the Ministry of Sea Transport now used this list to go round boatyards, particularly up the Thames, and begin commandeering these vessels. What would become known as the 'Little Ships of Dunkirk' would soon pass into legend, but at that moment, few of their owners knew what was going on. At least one allegedly reported his boat as stolen, personally pursuing it as far as Teddington Lock before discovering precisely who was doing the 'stealing'.

The desperate need for these little ships was further emphasised that evening when Captain Bill Tennant, newly arrived at Bastion 32 as Senior Naval Officer Dunkirk, ordered all troops and ships to head for the beaches, believing bombing had made the port untenable. Realising later that night that the 1,400-yard-long harbour breakwater, known as the East Mole, was untouched, Tennant ordered the 1,162-ton MV *Queen of the Channel* to tie up alongside to test the ability of the structure to withstand the simultaneous stresses of both ships tied up, and of large numbers of men packed four-abreast on its walkway. Remarkably, despite not having been designed for it, the Mole held, and *Queen of the Channel* departed at 0400 with 950 troops. Half an hour later, Tennant reopened Dunkirk, ordering all ships to head for the East Mole. The destroyer HMS *Vimy* arrived first, just 15 minutes later, leaving with another 613 troops. It was a vital improvisation,

MV *Queen of the Channel*. The 1,162-ton cross-Channel passenger ferry was requisitioned as a troopship, took part in the Boulogne operation before Dunkirk, and was bombed and sunk on the way home after proving ships could use the East Mole.

British troops boarding assorted vessels alongside the East Mole at Dunkirk, perhaps the place most critical to the success of Operation *Dynamo*.

for a scant 7,669 men had been evacuated on that first full day, far short of the totals needed even for Ramsay's modest initial aim of 45,000. Thanks to use of the Mole and additional ships, on the 28th that total grew to 17,804.

Among the new arrivals that day was a 2,156-ton French Navy sloop. Designed primarily for colonial service, *Savorgnan de Brazza* came equipped with communications and accommodation for an admiral and his staff. Aboard was the First World War submariner Rear Admiral Marcel Landriau, who had been appointed to command the Pas-de-Calais Flotilla, an ad-hoc collection of the large, 3,000-ton super-destroyers *Épervier* and *Léopard*, seven smaller destroyers, and approximately 200 other craft that would form the French contribution to Operation *Dynamo*, working under Ramsay. The First World War veteran battleships *Courbet* and *Paris*, reactivated from training duties in a remarkable 96 hours, also arrived at Cherbourg under a plan to use their huge guns to support a breakout by the Allied armies from the Dunkirk pocket (though this was, in the end, aborted).

This day, 28 May, also saw the end of another ally. The Belgian Army, under the direct command of King Leopold III, surrendered. After their warning, the British and French were prepared and had moved to protect their flank, but the loss of a 650,000-strong army was still a blow. Despite this, however, Belgium would still contribute 45 trawlers to Operation *Dynamo*, four of which would be lost in the process of evacuating 3,464 men.

The 29th would be critical in several ways, not least because although initial expectations had been that the evacuation would already be over, the defences of the Dunkirk pocket were still holding. Crucially, so too was the weather, any break in which could have brought the evacuation, particularly from the beaches, to a grinding halt. However,

Dunkirk's East Mole. Around two thirds of those evacuated made their way along along it to board the ships for safe evacuation to Britain.

Among those evacuated from the East Mole on 28 May were Major Akbar Khan and the 299 Royal Indian Army Service Corps mule handlers who had made it to Dunkirk (their mules were given to locals), some of whom can be seen here on exercise in Britain in November 1940.

The Kriegsmarine's motor torpedo boats, known as *Schnellboots* or *S-boots* (Enemy, or E-boats to the British), were 107 feet long, carrying two 21-inch torpedoes and two 20mm cannon, and proved deadly opponents in the Channel throughout the war.

it would be Operation *Dynamo*'s deadliest day, showing the range of threats facing the evacuees and their rescuers. It began in the earliest hour with the Kriegsmarine's deadly motor torpedo boats known as 'Schnellboots' or 'S-boots' ('enemy' or 'E-boats' to the British). Small, fast and heavily armed, they posed a formidable threat in the enclosed waters of the Channel, and at 0045 on the 29th the trail of two torpedoes from Lieutenant Willem Zimmerman's *S-30* emerged from the darkness 150 yards off the starboard bow of the destroyer HMS *Wakeful*. Despite the best efforts of Commander Ralph Fisher to evade, one struck home, causing the destroyer to split in half, sinking in seconds. *Wakeful*'s boats, with the help of others, had just loaded their ship with 650 men from the beaches at Bray. Now trapped below, only one would survive, along with 25 from *Wakeful*'s crew of 110.

Two hours later, another destroyer, HMS *Grafton*, arrived on the scene, similarly loaded with around 800 troops from Bray. A torpedo from Lieutenant Hans-Bernard Michalowski's U-boat, *U-62*, then slammed into the stern, breaking it off. In the confusion, *Grafton*, whose captain, Commander Cecil Robinson, had been killed in the attack, and the minesweeper HMS *Lydd*, which had also been assisting with rescue efforts, opened fire on a small vessel nearby, assuming it was another E-boat. *Lydd's* captain, Lieutenant Commander Rodolph Haig, then set course to ram the 'enemy'. Tragically, however, it turned out to be the trawler *Comfort*, which had just picked up 16 of *Wakeful's* survivors. This horrifying mistake would not be discovered until after *Lydd's* bow had cut *Comfort* in two. Some of *Comfort's* survivors, who tried to escape by leaping from the shattered trawler's decks to *Lydd's*, were also shot by Haig's men who stood ready to repel boarders. Fisher and four of his crew survived, sunk for a second time in as many hours, only this time, by their own side. Judged beyond sensible salvage efforts, *Grafton* was scuttled soon after, joining *Comfort* and *Wakeful* on the seabed.

Perhaps the main threat came from the air, however. Designed mainly to support the army, the Luftwaffe in mid-1940 was not particularly good at attacking ships at sea, lacking in both equipment, such as torpedoes, and training. Nonetheless, with their excellent Junkers Ju 87 and Ju 88 dive bombers to the fore, they remained a danger, particularly to stationary or slow-moving ships off beaches or in ports. This was precisely the scenario that occurred on the afternoon of the 29th, as no fewer than 14 British and French vessels of various sizes gathered inside Dunkirk harbour, with a number of others off the beaches.

In four air raids on the harbour, HMS *Grenade*, ablaze after two hits, was abandoned and towed out of the way lest the wreck block the Mole or harbour entrance, exploding some hours later as the fire reached the ship's magazines. The Manx packets *Fenella* and *King Orry* also sank after taking hits, *Fenella* almost immediately, *King Orry* some hours later when the crew attempted to sail their wounded ship home. Fellow Manx packet *Mona's Queen* had also been lost in just two minutes, after striking a mine earlier that morning while bringing drinking water to the troops on the beaches – a crucial, if unheralded, job in a port city whose amenities and

HMS *Grenade*, a 1,854-ton G Class destroyer. Skippered by Commander Richard Boyle, *Grenade* took part in the Norway Campaign prior to Dunkirk, and was credited with evacuating 1,000 men before being bombed and sunk in the harbour.

infrastructure would have been wildly overstretched by the numbers of evacuees, even without the bombing.

A number of ships in the harbour were also badly damaged. The French destroyer *Mistral* fell victim to a bomb that hit the quayside it was tied to, while HMS *Jaguar*, one of the Royal Navy's latest and most powerful destroyers, took a near miss that blew a large hole in the port side at the waterline. Both ships survived and sailed home, but neither took any further part in the evacuation.

The story was much the same off the beaches that afternoon, as the destroyers HMS *Greyhound*, HMS *Intrepid* and HMS *Saladin* were similarly damaged by the blast of near misses. They were, unfortunately, joined in rather more prosaic circumstances by HMS *Mackay* and HMS *Montrose*, which ran aground and collided with a tug, respectively. HMS *Gracie Fields*, HMS *Waverley* and HMS *Crested Eagle* – all converted civilian paddle-steamers requisitioned by the navy at the outbreak of war, and all loaded with troops – were hit and sunk off the beaches in those afternoon raids too. In some respects, however, perhaps the most remarkable and significant loss on the 29th was the SS *Clan Macalister*.

At 6,787 tons, the Clan Line cargo steamer was nearly twice the size of any other British ship taking part in the evacuation, but size was not the ship's only distinguishing feature. As the steamer arrived off the beaches that morning, the crew quickly began unloading their unusual cargo, courtesy of a small, tri-service organisation known as the 'Inter-Services Training and Development Centre'. Established at Eastney in 1938 to study amphibious operations and develop the necessary equipment and techniques, it was quickly realised that the new Assault, and Motor Landing Craft they had developed to get troops and equipment from ships onto beaches could probably do the reverse rather well too. By May 1940, only around 20 had been built, however, and four had been assigned to the Norwegian campaign, making their debut in the Allied landings at Bjerkvik two weeks earlier. Eight more, their crews led by Commander R.A. Cassidi, were loaded aboard *Clan Macalister*. Two were damaged on arrival while being hoisted out over the ship's side, but the remaining six performed sterling work, even after the loss of their mother-ship to Luftwaffe bombs at 1630. Still burning, *Clan Macalister*

Allied troops awaiting evacuation to transports and destroyers lying off the beaches at Dunkirk.

remained visible throughout the coming days, a conveniently distracting target for a number of other Luftwaffe attacks, much to the relief of other ships still working off the beaches.

Despite the painful losses, however, an astonishing 47,310 men had been evacuated, 33,558 from the harbour and 13,752 from the beaches. This was more in a single day than had been anticipated from the entire operation. It was later estimated that 10,000 more could have been rescued that day too, but for another communications mix-up and blackout that led to the harbour again being mistakenly declared closed for most of the night, pushing ships out to the beaches, once more dramatically slowing down the rate at which they could load evacuees.

For an evacuation like Dunkirk to succeed, a smooth flow of the largest possible number of ships arriving and leaving the harbour and beaches was called for. This meant essentially working to a timetable, loading as fully and quickly as possible by a constant flow of men up the Mole, or off the beaches via the boats and other little ships, followed by unloading at the receiving ports and refuelling and rearming as necessary for the next trip. This way, the greatest number of men could be brought back from France in the shortest possible time, but it had to work like clockwork, needing a high degree of organisation and communication both ashore and afloat. This would have been extremely difficult even in more peaceful circumstances, but in the face of intense enemy action, Operation *Dynamo* was desperately susceptible to disruptions of all kinds, particularly at the loading end, working through the single, badly damaged port that was Dunkirk.

Not a moment too soon, therefore, Ramsay had decided to seriously increase both the command team at Dunkirk and communications with Tennant and his men ashore there. Consequently, a large naval wireless set, with operators, was dispatched to Tennant that evening to try to avoid further communications blackouts. Seventy officers and men to act as beach parties travelled too, along with Frederic Wake-Walker who, as Rear Admiral Dover, was effectively Ramsay's deputy. Wake-Walker's task was to take command of the ever-expanding armada off the French and Belgian coasts and bring a greater level of organisation to it, and he began assessing the situation as soon as he stepped aboard the flagship Ramsay had assigned to him, Lieutenant Commander John Temple's minesweeper HMS *Hebe*, at 0100 on the 30th.

The choice of *Hebe* was a curious one, for unlike Landriau's *Savorgnan de Brazza*, *Hebe* lacked the space and communications equipment to act as flagship, resulting in Wake-Walker simply not receiving a number of vital signals. Worse, the ship had not even been excused evacuation duties, spending a significant part of the morning stationary, loading troops, before sailing for Britain, which forced Wake-Walker to shift his flag to the destroyer HMS *Windsor*. Here, he faced the same situation, having to shift again to HMS *Worcester*, then HMS *Express*, before the end of the day. Inevitably, he requested Ramsay assign him a flagship with suitable facilities, boarding *Keith* (now commanded by Captain Edward Berthon, after Simpson's death at Boulogne) the following morning. As lead ship of the 19th Destroyer Flotilla, *Keith*

HMS *Keith* an 1,821-ton B Class destroyer leader, key among Wake-Walker's many flagships at Dunkirk. *Keith* took part in the delivery of the BEF and evacuations from the Netherlands as well as Boulogne, and was credited with evacuating 1,200 men from Dunkirk.

had most of the space and communications Wake-Walker needed and had been taken off evacuation duties, removing the disruption of repeated ship transfers and enabling him to move quickly between port and beaches to exercise direct command as necessary. Surprisingly, however, when *Keith* was bombed and sunk on the morning of 1 June, Wake-Walker found himself aboard the motor torpedo boat MTB *102*, which was fast, of course, but at just 70 feet long had next to no space or communications facilities. Nonetheless, he remained aboard for most of the remainder of the evacuation, briefly switching to the similar motor anti-submarine boat MA/SB *10* on 2–3 June, before returning for the last day.

Though entirely coincidental, Wake-Walker making such a small vessel the flagship of the operation was wonderfully symbolic of an event that had occurred just a few hours before that would shape perceptions of the evacuation ever after. On the evening of the 31st, on one of his frequent trips from the beaches to the harbour, ironically to make enquiries about the perpetually pressured situation concerning the suitability of boats for the beaches, the admiral and everyone else on *Keith*'s bridge got the answer they were looking for in the most emphatic fashion imaginable. Before them lay an astonishing sight: a vast procession of small vessels of all kinds – tugs, trawlers, barges, lifeboats, fire-boats and all manner of working vessels – mixed with pleasure craft of all shapes and sizes, from rowing boats to yachts. The frantic work of Ramsay, Preston and those under their command to find, gather, organise, and in many cases crew this armada was now paying off. The 'little ships' had arrived.

They were desperately needed. Enemy action, swamping by desperate troops, surf, and accidents – from groundings and ramming to sometimes simply being allowed to drift away after the last soldier stepped off – had caused worrying losses to the flotilla of ships' boats, schuyts and other vessels that had been working the beaches from the start. There had never been enough either, despite best efforts to replace and reinforce throughout the first days. The little ships had also arrived just in time to take advantage of one of the more remarkable innovations of the evacuation. A wealth of British Army lorries that had to be destroyed anyway were now gathered at Dunkirk, so at low tide on the morning of the 30th the Royal Engineers had driven a number of them out beyond the tidelines at Bray and La Panne, parking them nose to tail and strapping wooden decking to their roofs. Though unable to take vessels of any great size, these two makeshift piers were the equivalent of the East Mole for the little ships, dramatically speeding up the task of loading men to ferry to the bigger ships offshore.

Ships were getting a lot better at loading too, with destroyers able to routinely load 600 men from the harbour in around 20 minutes. 'Remember your pals, boys!' went the cry. 'The quicker you get on board, the more of them will be saved!' A total of 68,014 men were evacuated from Dunkirk the day the little ships arrived. Another 64,429 followed on 1 June, including Gort himself, who had handed command of the remainder of the BEF in France to Major General Harold Alexander and sailed for Dover aboard MA/SB 6 just before dawn. These were the two most successful days of the operation, and they needed to be, as it was becoming increasingly obvious that the defensive perimeter

Troops of the Royal Ulster Rifles awaiting evacuation from one of the improvised lorry piers at high tide on 1 June 1940.

around Dunkirk would not hold much longer, and on the 1st the Luftwaffe and Kriegsmarine stepped up their attacks once more. *Keith* was, of course, one of the first to be lost to bombing that morning, along with *Skipjack*, to be followed by the destroyers HMS *Basilisk*, HMS *Havant* and the French *Foudroyant*, among others.

'For all the good you chaps seem to be doing over here you might just as well stay on the ground!' was the accusation from an unknown army major that greeted Pilot Officer Alan Deere, a young New Zealand pilot from 54 Squadron who landed his damaged Supermarine Spitfire fighter on the beach on the 29th. Unsurprisingly, given the bombing suffered by those on the beaches, in the harbour and manning the defences in Dunkirk, this was a question that many wanted to ask of the RAF, especially when it seemed that virtually the only aircraft to be seen in the skies above them were German. Yet from the RAF's perspective, the pace of operations had been ferocious. They would fly more than 2,700 sorties over the course of the evacuation, in which a number of future, famous aces experienced some of their first combat missions, most flying the Spitfires that had so far been held back from the fighting in France by Dowding's maintenance of the home defences. Alongside Deere, who had shot down his first German aircraft over Calais on 23 May, South African Flight Lieutenant Adolph 'Sailor' Malan of 74 Squadron had shot down his first over Dunkirk on the 21st, Flight Lieutenant Robert Stanford-Tuck of 92 Squadron opened his account over Dunkirk on the same day as Deere, while Flight Lieutenant Douglas Bader of 222 Squadron claimed one on 1 June.

The bombers had been busy too. Wing Commander Basil Embry of 107 Squadron was shot down on the 27th in his Bristol Blenheim, attacking a German column heading for Dunkirk. Wounded in the leg, he made a dramatic escape through German lines to the south of France, finding his way to Gibraltar ten weeks later. Some of the heavier Hampden,

Wellington and Whitley squadrons were also temporarily withdrawn from the new strategic bombing campaign against Germany for the duration of the evacuation, to hit roads and bridges approaching Dunkirk as well as supply lines and other targets in northern France, such as Bergues and elsewhere at night.

A number of notable faces also populated the naval air squadrons who were supporting the evacuation as part of Air Chief Marshal Sir Frederick Bowhill's RAF Coastal Command. The piratically red-bearded Lieutenant Commander Charles Evans commanded the Blackburn Skua fighter/dive bombers of 806 Naval Air Squadron (NAS). Along with their sister squadron, 801 NAS, which counted a Royal Marine lieutenant named Ron Hay among its pilots, 806 NAS joined the RAF's Spitfires and Hurricanes in trying to ward off the Luftwaffe. The Skua was a poor fighter, however, so its qualities as a dive bomber were rather more in demand, most notably in 801's raid on German forces at Nieuport in Belgium. Naval strike squadrons, flying the Fairey Swordfish torpedo/bomber, took on a variety of missions. 812 NAS, with Canadian Lieutenant Roy Baker-Faulkner, attacked artillery and tanks in the Dunkirk–Bergues area on the 29th, laid mines off the Dutch coast and bombed the Vlaardingen oil tanks near Rotterdam on the 31st. The loss of five aircraft that day brought Lieutenant Commander Eugene Esmond to command 825 NAS, while Lieutenant Charles Lamb, a young pilot with 815 NAS, was deeply moved by the scene that unfolded beneath his Swordfish. His experience would lead him to play a crucial role in commemorating Operation *Dynamo* after the war. At that moment, however, he and his squadron were busy patrolling to counter the deadly E-boat attacks.

Dowding had his aircraft primarily flying patrol lines inland, beyond sight of the beaches and ships lying off them, trying to intercept and break up Luftwaffe attacks before

Chain Home radar masts at Swingate, near Dover Castle, completed in 1936 as part of a growing network along Britain's southern and eastern coasts to detect aircraft long before they reached Britain.

they reached the evacuation area. This was perhaps the key reason that ground forces thought that the RAF was not being much help, as they were out of sight. Another was that despite its undoubted sophistication, and the people within it, on the ground and in the air, straining every last sinew, the integrated air defence system Dowding not only commanded but had helped create was working beyond its limits. It had been designed to defend Britain, not northern France. The patrol lines his fighters were flying therefore lay at and beyond the range of the famous Chain Home early warning radar stations on the British coast. As a consequence, the network of air controllers at the heart of the system lacked sufficient warning to be able to scramble and surge numbers into the right place at the right time, as would happen with such great success during the Battle of Britain. Exhausting and inefficient though it was, this then left the fighters trying to maintain a constant presence on the patrol lines if they were to have a hope of protecting the evacuation. Matters were not helped by a cumbersome command structure, divided between Ramsay at Dover Castle, Dowding at Bentley Priory, Bowhill at Eastbury Park and Portal at High Wycombe, while Blount at RAF Hawkinge was still handling co-operation between these commands and what remained of the BEF on the ground at Dunkirk.

Ramsay tried to counter locally, putting ships with powerful anti-aircraft armament, such as the anti-aircraft cruiser HMS *Calcutta* and Polish destroyer ORP *Błyskawica*, out into the evacuation routes to provide additional firepower against both aircraft and E-boats. These ships had some success, but there was no way of bringing the two parts of the defences together tactically, even if anybody had wished to. Lacking

The operations room at 11 Group Headquarters RAF Uxbridge, which helped direct the Battle of Britain air defence, much as they had tried to do just a few months before at Dunkirk, is now open to the public as a museum.

radar, the right radios, or trained fighter control personnel and facilities, they had no real picture of what aircraft might have been in the area or any way of co-ordinating efforts with those that were. The Royal Navy had only just begun experimenting with such things in April and efforts were concentrated on the fleet's aircraft carriers, which were operating off Norway. Ships and troops therefore mainly had to rely on their own guns and hope that passing fighters heading to and from their patrol lines might be in the right place at the right time when the Luftwaffe attacks got through.

After the successes of 31 May–1 June, rescue figures for the remaining days of the evacuation dropped dramatically to around 26,000 per day. German air power and particularly artillery, which was now in range of both the port itself and the sailing routes in increasing numbers, was making daytime operations too dangerous to contemplate. Ramsay therefore ordered all vessels to leave the evacuation area before dawn on 2 June. Abrial objected, but Ramsay remained firm, signalling to his vessels later that morning that the night would require maximum effort. Remarkably, by 2330, they

HMS *Calcutta*, seen before the modernisation that breathed new life into a hitherto obsolescent warship.

had done it. The remaining 3,460 men boarded the troop ships *King George V* and *St Helier*, while Alexander boarded the destroyer HMS *Venomous* after a final, personal tour of the port and beaches. Tennant, aboard Wake-Walker's MTB *102*, was now able to send the famous signal 'BEF evacuated'.

This was not the end of Operation *Dynamo*, however, for there remained, of course, the none-too-small matter of the French Army that had fought hard to hold the perimeter for far longer than anticipated to allow the BEF to escape. Many had already been evacuated, not least by Landriau's Pas-de-Calais Flotilla, but up to 65,000 remained in the Dunkirk pocket, including Abrial himself. Unfortunately, a delay in getting French troops to the harbour to follow their British brethren onto the waiting Allied ships meant an estimated 10,000 fewer than anticipated would be rescued before operations paused again at daybreak.

By this point, Ramsay was acutely aware that most of his ships' crews were approaching the limits of physical endurance. A number of ships had been withdrawn from the operation already due to fatigue. Nevertheless, he resolved to make one final effort, warning the Admiralty that anything more would require fresh ships and crews. This, combined with the efforts of the French troops themselves to evacuate on any of the large number of local small boats that were in the harbour that final night led to chaotic scenes and a number of collisions and groundings, including the French Navy motor torpedo boat VTB *25* carrying Abrial, which struck some underwater wreckage and had to be towed to Dover by the destroyer HMS *Malcolm*. Last to leave at 0340, some ten minutes after the Germans had begun their morning artillery bombardment, was the destroyer HMS *Shikari* with General Robert Barthélemy and 383 of his men, the last of 26,175 to be evacuated that day. Barthélemy warned *Shikari*'s captain, Commander Hugh Richardson, that there were at least 12,000 French troops still in Dunkirk. The true number, however, was closer to 40,000 exhausted men whose ammunition supplies were now gone. It was considered unlikely that this battered force could hold out for another night, and with the evacuation flotilla also near breaking point, Ramsay and Abrial agreed. The signal 'Operation *Dynamo* now completed' was transmitted at 1423 on 4 June.

SS *King George V*: the 789-ton Clyde passenger steamer had been requisitioned as a troopship, taking part in the Netherlands, Calais and Boulogne operations, before bringing 4,300 out of Dunkirk. *King George V* was scrapped after a fire at Cardiff in 1981.

THE SHIPS

O PERATION *DYNAMO* WAS an immense undertaking involving all three armed services at sea, in the air and on land, but it is with ships, and little ships in particular, that the evacuation of Dunkirk is most associated. More than 800 vessels, naval and civilian, of varying sizes, took part, which in some respects begs the question, what were the 'little ships'? The image frequently conjured by those words can tend towards the mainly civilian yachts and pleasure craft that make up the bulk of the members of the Association of Dunkirk Little Ships, yet it can quite easily be said that the answer is all of them. *Courbet* and *Paris* were the only two battleships in the Channel, and they were not called to the evacuation. Nor would any of the great transatlantic liners appear off the beaches. Despite the potentially enormous numbers of men such big ships might have carried on each trip, as well as being extremely tempting targets when stationary, their great size would have left them at risk of grounding off the shallow beaches, or too far away to quickly load from the smaller vessels. Furthermore, putting ships of around 1,500 tons against the untested East Mole had been risky enough. The massive 25,000-ton bulk of either of the two French battleships, for example, would in all likelihood have destroyed that vital structure, even if they had been able to get close enough to tie up alongside.

The largest warship to take part in the evacuation was the 4,290-ton First World War vintage C Class anti-aircraft cruiser HMS *Calcutta*, commanded by Captain Dennis Lees. Built at Vickers' yard at Barrow-in-Furness, but commissioned too late to see action in the First World War, *Calcutta* had been taken in hand at Chatham for modernisation in 1938 after a career spent abroad

on the North American and South African stations, and then in reserve. Emerging from refit just weeks before the start of the war, with a powerful new anti-aircraft armament, *Calcutta*, along with similarly converted sister ships HMS *Cairo*, HMS *Coventry* and HMS *Curlew*, was crewed mainly by reservists from HMS *President*, a former First World War Q-Ship moored at Blackfriars on the Thames that served as the headquarters ship for the London Division of the Royal Navy Volunteer Reserve.

HMS *President*, the 1,300-ton Flower Class Q-Ship commissioned in 1918 as HMS *Saxifrage* but renamed upon becoming the drill ship of the London Royal Navy Reserve in 1922. Decommissioned in 1988, *President* awaits restoration at Chatham.

Arriving at Dunkirk fresh from the Norwegian campaign and the evacuation of Åndalsnes, *Calcutta* was arguably underutilised during Operation *Dynamo*. Bringing 1,856 men home was obviously no small matter, while the ship's heavy anti-aircraft firepower protected the transit of countless others and was much appreciated. Yet what really might have made a difference was *Calcutta*'s command and communication capabilities, which, as the only cruiser involved, were the finest to be found off the beaches. It is at least slightly surprising that Ramsay did not assign *Calcutta* to Wake-Walker as flagship, or, if *Calcutta* could not be spared, that the slightly larger, more modern *Arethusa* and *Galatea* were held at Sheerness after their efforts supporting the forces at Calais.

With Operation *Dynamo* complete, along with a host of other Dunkirk veterans, *Calcutta* helped evacuate the remainder of the BEF from France's western ports, although this ended in tragedy for the cruiser. Once repaired, *Calcutta* transferred to the Mediterranean, escorting a number of convoys to the besieged island of Malta and taking part in the evacuation of Greece, before finally succumbing to Luftwaffe air attack off Alexandria on 1 June 1941, while covering yet another famous Allied evacuation, this time from Crete. None of the four sisters crewed from HMS *President* survived the war. One near sister still exists, however. HMS *Caroline*, an earlier version of the C Class cruiser and the last survivor of the 1916 Battle of Jutland, is now open to the public as a museum ship in Belfast, Northern Ireland, as part of the National Museum of the Royal Navy.

Destroyers were the most numerous type of fighting ship at Dunkirk. The great workhorses of the world's navies, these small, fast, manoeuvrable ships were armed with guns to take on ships and aircraft, depth charges to take on submarines, and torpedoes that made them a threat to even the greatest battleships. Built to fight, with cramped passageways, hatches and living spaces, and much space dedicated to armament and machinery, these ships were far from ideal transporters of people. Nonetheless, the navy set to the task with gusto, cramming their army brethren into every nook and cranny they possibly could that did not interfere with the operation of the guns or the engines, or the stability of the ship. What made the 20-minute loading rate achieved in the latter stages so remarkable was that it required the sailors to direct as many of the soldiers as possible below decks, deep into the bowels of the ship. Not unnaturally, of course, the prospect of being trapped in a confined, unfamiliar, and wildly overcrowded space, below the waterline of a ship, with few exits, was not entirely appealing to more than

Londoners of the Royal Navy Reserve who would be drafted from HMS *President* on the outbreak of war to crew HMS *Calcutta*, relaxing by one of the ship's guns in more peaceful times.

HMS *Caroline*, commissioned in 1914 and converted into a drill ship for Ulster's Royal Navy reservists in 1924. Not considered worth modernising, *Caroline* was finally decommissioned as a training ship in 2011 for preservation by the National Museum of the Royal Navy.

a few of the exhausted soldiers, some of whom had spent the last few weeks being shot at, bombed and shelled. In those circumstances, salvation could turn into death in a few short moments, were the ship to be hit. Nonetheless, most quietly accepted direction below, grateful for food, water, rest and the chance to get home. The Royal Navy put no fewer than 41 destroyers into Operation *Dynamo*, the French Navy 14, the Polish Navy one. Nine – six British and three French – would not survive. A number of others suffered varying degrees of damage, but together they carried by far the greatest number of troops to safety of any type of ship, with a total of 102,843.

About half of the Royal Navy destroyers taking part were, like *Calcutta*, older, smaller ships, built in the last years of the First World War. At around 1,100 tons, with 4-inch guns, the majority of these S, V and W Class ships had been relegated to the Reserve Fleet by the 1930s and were only reactivated due to the wartime need for destroyers to escort convoys and for coastal defence. The remainder were primarily the inter-war A, B, E, G, H and I classes, of around 1,350 tons with 4.7-inch guns, including one of Wake-Walker's more significant flagships, the B Class flotilla leader HMS *Keith*. Built through the 1930s, these ships had been the mainstays of the fleet in the years before the war, playing a full part in the evacuation of civilians from cities like Barcelona, and the escorting of merchant ships and anti-submarine patrols during the Spanish Civil War. Worn out after hard wars, particularly escorting the vital Atlantic and Arctic convoys, those that survived were quickly scrapped, including the most successful destroyer at Dunkirk, the Scott Class flotilla leader HMS *Malcolm*, commanded by Captain Thomas Halsey of the 16th Destroyer flotilla, which, having helped out with the evacuation of the Netherlands, brought 5,851 men out of Dunkirk.

Among the newest, and most powerful, destroyers taking part were the three brand-new, 1,800-ton J Class ships HMS *Jackal*, HMS *Jaguar* and HMS *Javelin*, armed with six 4.7-inch guns in three twin turrets, built to a new hull design that became the template for virtually all British destroyers built during the war, and the similarly armed, big 1,975-ton

HMS *Javelin* approaching Dunkirk during the evacuation. On 29 November 1940, *Javelin* survived the loss of both bow and stern in battle off Plymouth, returning to action a year later – testament to the remarkable strength of the new design.

Polish destroyer ORP *Błyskawica*, built in Britain by J. Samuel White at Cowes on the Isle of Wight as part of Poland's pre-war rearmament programme. Rescuing 1,400 men from Dunkirk, only *Javelin* would survive the war out of the three J Class, serving off Norway, in the Atlantic, the Mediterranean, the Indian Ocean and the Arctic as well as D-Day, to be scrapped at West of Scotland Shipbreakers at Troon in June 1949.

Błyskawica had been commissioned in November 1937 and sailed for Poland's main naval base at Gdynia, making the return journey to Britain in tragic circumstances just under two years later, joining the most modern and powerful units of the Polish Navy. A similar arrangement to the one that would bring the Dutch Navy to Britain the following year, the 'Peking Plan' had been agreed on 26 August 1939 and was executed just three days later. *Błyskawica,* sister ship ORP *Grom* and the French-built destroyer ORP *Burza* made their daring escape from Gdynia, past the German forces they knew to be massing for the attack. They arrived at Leith to join forces with the Royal Navy on the evening of 1 September, with the war against their homeland now well underway.

Błyskawica arrived at Dunkirk fresh from the Norwegian campaign, like *Calcutta, Javelin* and others, but unusually among the destroyers taking part, would end the evacuation with no tally of rescued men, having been assigned solely to provide anti-aircraft and anti-submarine protection. More than a few would owe their survival to Lieutenant Commander Stanisław Nahorski and his crew, including the 506 men rescued from the beaches at La Panne by HMS *Greyhound* on 28 May who were towed out of the danger area by *Błyskawica* when the British destroyer was crippled by Luftwaffe bombs.

Błyskawica had an extremely busy war, escorting convoys in the Atlantic and the Mediterranean, including the fabled Operation *Pedestal* convoy to relieve Malta in 1942. Refitted with a new main armament of eight 4-inch, dual-purpose guns in 1941, the ship famously defended Cowes when the Luftwaffe blitzed the

ORP *Błyskawica*, and sister ship ORP *Grom*, were valuable vessels, not only because of their fighting power, but because their British design and construction made it easy to update them in the UK after the fall of the Continent.

town in May 1942 and, in the Battle of Ushant, helped take on a German destroyer flotilla that was trying to attack the Allied invasion fleet off Normandy, three days after D-Day. Returning to Poland after the war, *Błyskawica* was finally decommissioned and preserved as a museum ship at Gdynia in 1976, the last of the 56 destroyers to take part in Operation *Dynamo*, or indeed any of the major evacuations of that summer of 1940, to survive both the war and the scrappers' torch.

Minesweepers were another, extremely important, group of warships to take part in the evacuation of Dunkirk, for as well as transporting men from the harbour and beaches, theirs was also the hugely dangerous task of clearing the routes through the lethal minefields that littered the Channel. These ships had to inch their way among the massive, steel-cased explosive charges, anchored to the seabed, lying, waiting, just below the surface for unsuspecting ships to pass, exploding with hull-shattering power at the slightest touch (or even without, if dealing with magnetic mines). Many of the mines they faced were their own. HMS *Adventure* and HMS *Plover* had begun laying the first Allied minefields in the Dover Strait eight days after war was declared, and many more had been laid since. These posed a major hazard to ships involved in the evacuation if they were unfortunate enough to stray off course, and some had to be cleared, particularly before Route 'X' could be declared safe to use. Then, of course, there was the constant need to counter German efforts.

The 38 minesweepers that took part were a curiously mixed group. There were, of course, two French vessels, *Commandant Delage* and *L'Impétueuse*, which between them evacuated 2,038 men, along with the combination of ships built towards the end of the First World War, such as the 710-ton, Hunt Class HMS *Lydd*, whose Dunkirk experience was particularly double-edged, with the desperate tragedy of the sinking of *Comfort* alongside the evacuation of 1,502 men over the course of five trips to both the East Mole and the beaches and back. Of the more modern ships, HMS *Halcyon* and HMS *Skipjack* exemplified the twin duties of the minesweepers by evacuating a combined 3,136 men, as well as clearing the vital Route 'X'. *Halcyon* survived the war, but hit by no fewer than five bombs early on 1 June, *Skipjack* would be among the five minesweepers lost during the evacuation. Wake-Walker's initial flagship HMS *Hebe* survived the evacuation, rescuing 1,140 men, until bomb damage and a spate of physical collapses from fatigue among the crew caused the ship's withdrawal from operations on 1 June. Tragically, *Hebe* later sank just four minutes after striking two mines while clearing Bari

Bourrasque, a 1,900-ton Bourrasque Class destroyer commissioned in 1926. The vessel was hit by German artillery on 30 May 1940, being forced into an Allied minefield, where it sank while evacuating 600 French troops from Dunkirk harbour.

harbour in Italy on 22 November 1943, highlighting the intense danger of their work.

Not all the Royal Navy's minesweepers were purpose-built warships, however. Always short of such vessels in war, the Admiralty had plans in place to requisition suitable vessels from civilian life, crew them with reservists, and put them to work in the role, much as they had during the First World War. Among the ships requisitioned for this were paddle steamers. Usually used in peacetime to ferry holidaymakers to coastal resort towns, and despite seeming desperately out of place in a mid-20th-century warzone, steamers were highly valued for their manoeuvrability and low-speed handling, crucial in minefields. One in particular, the 393-ton former Red Funnel Line steamer, HMS *Gracie Fields*, quickly became synonymous with the evacuation thanks to a famous BBC radio broadcast on 5 June. The popular broadcaster J.B. Priestley spoke of his pride in the *Gracie Fields*, which had been launched in 1936 at Thornycroft's by the star who gave the ship her name, 'for she was the glittering queen of our local line', and told of 'how the little holiday steamers made an excursion to hell and came back glorious'. Priestley's beloved *Gracie Fields* was, of course, among those that did not come back, falling victim to Luftwaffe bombs on the 29th, with 750 troops aboard. Others did make it back, however, such as HMS *Queen of Thanet* (remarkably, built as the Racecourse Class minesweeper HMS *Melton* in 1916 and converted to civilian pleasure steaming on the Medway in 1929, before returning to minesweeping in 1939), and returned to pleasure steaming after the war, before being progressively scrapped in the 1950s and 1960s as patterns of British holidaymaking changed and their commercial worth declined.

HMS *Medway Queen* and HMS *Princess Elizabeth* managed to escape this fate, however. The former, a product of Ailsa's Troon yard in 1924, officially rescued 3,064 in a remarkable seven trips to both harbour and beaches under the command of Lieutenant Thomas Cook (claims of up to

7,000 are made, which are not unfeasible given the chaotic nature of the operation and the available records). The ship then returned to the Medway cruise routes in 1947 until being laid up in 1963, thereafter becoming a nightclub and restaurant on the Isle of Wight until accidentally sinking in 1984. *Medway Queen* was purchased by the Medway Queen Preservation Society and returned once more to the Medway, beginning a long process of preservation that saw near loss again in 1997 and major restoration work at Bristol in 2008, before returning to Gillingham Pier in 2013. *Princess Elizabeth*, a 388-ton Red Funnel Line sister of *Gracie Fields*, built in 1927, returned to the Isle of Wight service in 1946, having rescued 1,673 men in four trips to Dunkirk. It was transferred to other routes on the south coast of England in 1958, after being superseded by newer vessels. Within just a few years, and despite a cinematic appearance as *Persevero II* in Disney's *In Search of the Castaways*, *Princess Elizabeth* was stripped of engines and other features, beginning a new life as a restaurant and event venue in a variety of different locations, including London, Paris and finally back to Dunkirk and another brush

Medway Queen was among the holiday steamers that had been requisitioned in 1939, being armed with a 12-pounder gun in the bow, minesweeping gear at the stern, and pressed into service as a minesweeper. She is now restored as a museum ship on the River Medway.

Princess Elizabeth, another holiday steamer, was pressed into service as a minesweeper, and is now restored and moored in Dunkirk as a floating restaurant.

with movie stardom in the 2017 film based on the evacuation.

Several other types of naval vessel took part in Operation *Dynamo* in small numbers, including sloops, such as the French *Savorgnan de Brazza*, which rescued no troops, but of course performed a vital role as Landriau's flagship. Seized at Portsmouth on 3 July 1940 as part of Operation *Catapult* – the remarkable, but tragic, British effort to neutralise the French Navy – and turned over to the Free French, *Savorgnan de Brazza* spent the rest of the war taking part in the battles for the French colonies in Africa and the Indian Ocean and resumed colonial patrol duties after the war until scrapping in 1957. Others, such as the brand new, 625-ton Dragonfly Class gunboats HMS *Locust* and HMS *Mosquito*, did join the evacuation efforts, rescuing 3,512 men between them, *Mosquito* becoming another loss in the air attacks on 1 June, though *Locust* survived Dieppe and D-Day, before being scrapped at Newport in 1968.

The Allies also employed small numbers of their own versions of the deadly E-boats. Descendants of the torpedo-carrying Coastal Motor Boats developed by Sir John Thornycroft and Lieutenants Anson, Bremner and Hampden in 1915, this new generation of motor torpedo boats was another private venture, this time by Commander Peter Du Cane, managing director and chief designer of the Portsmouth boat builder Vosper. The 68-foot, planing hull prototype Du Cane built in 1937 was quickly bought by the Admiralty and commissioned as MTB *102*, the design forming

VTB 24, part of the French flotilla that included VTB 25, which evacuated Admiral Abrial. Damaged at Dunkirk and captured by the British on 3 July 1940, VTB 24 spent the rest of the war with the Royal Navy.

the basis of a massive rebuilding programme for the Royal Navy's Coastal Forces for the forthcoming war. MTB *102*, of course, became Wake-Walker's main flagship after the loss of *Keith*. Lieutenant Christopher Dreyer's crew created a makeshift rear admiral's flag with red paint and a dishcloth, taking the admiral wherever he was needed, from harbour, to beaches, to Dover and back. Consequently, they were among the last to leave Dunkirk on 4 June. Only around 100 men would actually be evacuated aboard the 15 motor torpedo and anti-submarine boats that took part. Instead, they would mostly find employment countering their Kriegsmarine counterparts and as fast transports for senior commanders, with MA/SB *10* (a very similar design, created by Hubert Scott-Paine of the British Power

VTB 24 following conversion into the houseboat *Pelican*, a frequent use for surplus motor torpedo boats sold off after the end of the war.

Boat Company in Hythe) briefly taking MTB *102*'s place as flagship, MA/SB *6* bringing Gort out and the French VTB *25* (Scott-Paine's BPBC design sold to the French Navy) carrying Abrial out.

MTB *102* was not done with transporting higher command either, carrying Churchill and Supreme Allied Commander US Army General Dwight Eisenhower for their review of ships assembled for the D-Day landings on 5 June 1944. After the war, MTB *102* was sold into private hands, spending time as a private motor cruiser and houseboat, before being restored to seagoing condition by Kelso Films for the 1976 Hollywood film *The Eagle Has Landed*, starring Michael Caine. Acquired by the Suffolk-based MTB 102 Trust in 1996, the vessel remains seaworthy, taking part in commemorative events with the Association of Dunkirk Little Ships and others, as well as filming for television and movies such as the 2017 *Dunkirk*. Others had less certain fates; many of those that survived the war, such as MA/SB *10* (reclassified as MGB *10* in January 1941) were sold in 1945, along with many other Coastal Forces boats, to fates unknown, frequently being converted into yachts and houseboats. One example of Scott-Paine's

MTB *102* on the River Thames.

BPBC design, MGB *81*, built in 1942, has been restored and can be seen at the Portsmouth Historic Dockyard.

Along with the navy's destroyers, passenger vessels were, perhaps, the most important ships to take part in the evacuation of Dunkirk. The 56 present in various guises brought back 95,364 soldiers from the harbour and beaches. Virtually all were crewed by the civilians of the Merchant Navy, drawn from all corners of the British Empire and beyond, bar *King Orry*, *Lormont* and *Mona's Isle*, the three ships that had been taken into service as Armed Boarding Vessels – small passenger vessels given a couple of 4-inch guns and put to work intercepting and inspecting merchant ships to enforce the blockade of Germany. Even these ships tended to have plentiful numbers of Merchant Navy sailors, particularly engineers, aboard, working under naval discipline through a civilian contract scheme known as the T124. Many of the others had spent the preceding months transporting the BEF across the Channel in the first place. Eight were acting as hospital ships, with medical teams aboard, their suites and saloons converted into wards and operating theatres. Painted white, with vast red crosses on the side, they were supposed to be immune from attack, though this was not always observed.

HMHS *Worthing* was among the many ships that helped deliver the BEF to France in 1939 and helped bring them back in 1940. *Worthing* evacuated 600 casualties from Dunkirk harbour, but was damaged on 2 June.

NORMAN WILKINSON

These ships were both the best, and the worst, vessels to use for a mass evacuation of people, for they had multiple points of comparatively easy entry and exit, leading into wide corridors with minimal impairment by watertight bulkheads, and most of their volume was given over to relatively spacious living areas of various types. In essence, they were designed to load and carry passengers in large numbers, usually at a relatively reasonable speed, and everything about them was designed to facilitate this. The cargo vessels, designed primarily to move goods, were similarly open – unlike the cramped, heavily subdivided warships, much of the volume of which was dedicated to machinery, weapons and their magazines, and so on. Yet each of these advantages and qualities that allowed them to shift great masses of humanity efficiently could quickly become fatal flaws if disaster struck. They carried precious little armament and no protection, and in the event the ship was hit, fire and water could also take advantage of those broad, uninterrupted corridors, and spacious staterooms and saloons, to terrible effect.

The Admiralty had long kept lists of British flagged vessels thought to be of use in wartime. With a combination of boat davits that could handle a good number of Assault Landing Craft on a not-too-large hull, the 6,787-ton SS *Clan Macalister*, a cargo steamer built some ten years before for the Clan Line of Glasgow, was quickly requisitioned, loaded with these new boats, and dispatched to the beaches. Unlucky enough to be among the ten passenger vessels lost during Dunkirk, fatally bombed even before being fully loaded with evacuees, *Clan Macalister*'s capacity was never fully utilised, but the cargo of Assault Landing Craft would prove an invaluable contribution.

The capacities of other passenger vessels were used rather more fully, however. Officially, the most successful in terms of numbers evacuated was the 2,200-ton Manx Packet SS *Tynwald*. Built by Vickers Armstrong at Barrow-in-Furness and completed in 1937, *Tynwald* was requisitioned almost immediately by the Board of Trade as a troop transport to deliver the BEF to the Continent. Captain John Whiteway (relieved towards the end of the operation by Wilfred Qualtrough) and his crew of merchant mariners evacuated no fewer than 8,953 men from Dunkirk. The 4,950-ton Norwegian cargo ship MV *Hird*, which had been built in Glasgow in 1924, brought 3,500 back – more than any other non-British flagged vessel. Neither *Tynwald* nor *Hird* would see out the war, both being lost to submarines. Having been converted into an auxiliary anti-aircraft ship, *Tynwald* would be torpedoed by the Italian submarine *Argo* on 12 November 1942. *Hird* would be lost to a torpedo from U-65 off the Hebrides on 15 September 1940.

One of the largest contributions to the evacuation came from the fishing community, with 230 trawlers and drifters taking part – 113 from Britain, 72 from France and another 45 from Belgium – bringing a combined total of 28,709 out of Dunkirk. The great fishing fleets had long been sources of manpower for the navies of Europe, but the years before the

SS *Tynewald*, the most successful of the Merchant Navy troopships assigned to Operation *Dynamo*, passing the barely visible wreck of fellow Manx packet *King Orry* while approaching Dunkirk.

PREVIOUS
PAGES
Fishing boats of
the Association
of Dunkirk Little
Ships: the cockle
boat *Endeavour*;
lugger *Maid
Marion*; and
trawler *Caronia*.

Maid Marion, a
39-foot Cornish
lugger, remained
a working
trawler during
the war, and,
sailing too late to
join Operation
Dynamo, she was
instead assigned
to Operation
Cycle, evacuating
troops from
Le Havre.

First World War had seen a renewed emphasis on them as it became clear that their small vessels could make an impact in dealing with the new forms of naval warfare in the submarine and the mine. Their shallow drafts and equipment designed to deliver large nets into the water, tow slowly and then bring the nets back in, were of particular interest in minesweeping, which operated very similarly, only with equipment for cutting mine moorings, rather than nets. Consequently, many fishing boats would be requisitioned at the start of both world wars, armed, and put to work in this way. With plenty of reservists among the crews, many fishermen would continue to operate their own boats, only with naval rank. Used in a variety of roles, from evacuating troops to minesweeping to countering the U- and E-boats, 27 would be lost during the evacuation, among the highest casualties of the operation. As working boats, few survived the peace and the changing economics of the fishing industry. Those that did tend to be among the smaller vessels, such as the *Enterprise* and *Edward and Mary*, now at the Hastings Fishermen's Museum, and the 15-foot fishing boat *Tamzine*, built in 1937 by Brockman and Titcombe in Margate, the smallest vessel to take part in Operation *Dynamo*, acquired by the Imperial War Museum after the war and still on display at the museum's main site in London.

Other working vessels included tugs. Usually to be found in wartime assisting ships into

their berths in harbours (much as they would in peacetime), 40 would be employed at Dunkirk, both in the harbour role there and towing many of the smallest craft across the Channel and back, as well as helping to save those larger ships that had been damaged and crippled by enemy action. Collectively, they also brought 3,164 troops out of

Dunkirk. Three would be lost in the operation, but, once more, few survived the peace. The 110-foot *Challenge* was the last steam tug operating on the Thames in a commercial career that lasted from 1931 to 1974, becoming a museum ship at St Katherine's Dock in London. One of the first vessels to be rescued from neglect by the Dunkirk Little Ships Restoration Trust in 1993, *Challenge* has undergone considerable restoration and remains in the possession of the Trust, able to sail to commemorative events.

Endeavour, the 34-foot Cockle Bawley, now restored and owned by a charitable trust, remained a working fishing boat throughout the war, making the trip to Dunkirk with her civilian crew to help evacuate troops.

The 15-foot fishing boat *Tamzine*, built in 1937, and the smallest known vessel to have taken part in Operation *Dynamo* was acquired for the Imperial War Museum after the war.

With their shallow drafts, flat bottoms and considerable carrying capacity, barges seemed an ideal solution to trying to extract the large numbers of men from the beaches around Dunkirk; several would be requisitioned from the Thames and dispatched. Initially, the key source of these vessels for Operation *Dynamo* was the Netherlands or, more specifically, the schuyts that had escaped from that country before its surrender and had been gathered in London and Poole. Given Royal Navy crews, 40 of these schuyts with engines were among the first vessels sent across on 27 May. By the end of the operation on 4 June, they had evacuated 22,698 men, losing four of their number in the process. Spending the rest of the war working as harbour lighters, barges and cargo carriers in Britain, the schuyts were returned to commercial service in the Netherlands

The 110-foot steam tug *Challenge* not only took part in the Allied evacuation, but also the return, towing sections of the pre-fabricated Mulberry Harbour across the Channel to Normandy for D-Day in 1944.

Lucy Lavers, the 35-foot Aldeburgh Lifeboat was brand new when requisitioned to sail for Dunkirk. Finally retiring as a lifeboat in 1968, *Lucy Lavers* was restored in 2010.

after the war, their numbers dwindling over time due to replacement by more modern vessels. Those that escaped the scrapyard found new roles as houseboats and river cruisers, though it is believed that only two of the 40 that took part in Operation *Dynamo* still exist, including the *Amazone*. Based at Poole, *Amazone* was placed under the command of Lieutenant

Commander L.H. Phillips, rescuing 549 men. Now named *Welsh Liberty, Amazone* is a privately owned pleasure cruiser based in France.

Often forgotten, yet among the most crucial naval vessels, were the smallest utilised at Dunkirk. These were the ships' boats. Like other vessels of any size, warships carried a range of whalers, cutters, motorboats, picket boats and life-rafts hanging from davits at the ships' sides. Naturally, these played a vital role if the ship sank, but the boats were principally for transferring people between ships while at sea, or from ship

The 45-foot Newhaven Lifeboat *Stenoa* rescued 51 men from Dunkirk. Finally retiring as a lifeboat in 1959, *Stenoa* has been restored as a private yacht.

The 78-foot London Fire Boat *Massey Shaw* brought 106 men back from Dunkirk under the command of Sub-Officer A.J. May of the London Fire Brigade, who was awarded the Royal Navy's Distinguished Service Medal.

The last surviving RAF High Speed Air Sea Rescue Launch *102* on the River Thames. The vessel is of the same design as HSL *120*, which took part in the Dunkirk evacuation.

to shore in places where there was no port, or ports were too shallow or were otherwise unsuitable. This was, of course, the situation that faced the ships detailed to pick men up from the beaches, only on a scale few could possibly have imagined. Nonetheless, the ships' boats' crews set to their daunting task with a will, lowering their boats, sailing, rowing, or being towed to the beach, then loading the boats with troops and returning to the ship. The rescued men then climbed scramble-nets, ropes and rope-ladders up the ship's side, whereupon the boat would return to the beach for another load of men, repeating this process until the ship could hold no more, at which point the boats would be hoisted back aboard and the ship would turn for home. Filling a destroyer this way took hours, during which time the ship would largely be stationary and

The 92-foot sail barge *Pudge* sailed to Dunkirk skippered by Bill Watson of the London and Rochester Trading Company. Finally retiring from commercial life in 1968, *Pudge* has been restored and is owned by a charitable trust.

vulnerable under repeated Luftwaffe attack. Repeated losses through accidents, swamping and so on necessitated replacements from stores and even other ships under repair. For example, the motorboat and picket boat of the Home Fleet flagship, the battleship HMS *Nelson*, under repair

after striking a magnetic mine, brought 71 men back to Britain, as well as ferrying countless others to bigger ships. Despite this there were never enough boats working off the beaches, leading to the requisitioning of anything vaguely suitable, from the personal barges of Ramsay and the Admiral Superintendent Portsmouth (both of which would be lost), to the rather more radical solution of the Assault Landing Craft brought across by the *Clan Macalister*.

Designed by Thornycroft for Captain Loben Maund's Inter-Services Training and Development Centre, the prototype of

The 80-foot sail barge *Greta* had already been requisitioned in 1939 to carry ammunition out to warships in the Thames estuary and resumed that role after Dunkirk. Finally retiring from commercial life in the early 1960s, *Greta* has been restored as a houseboat.

A Royal Navy destroyer lowering one of its whalers in 1942, much as the vessels off the beaches of Dunkirk would have done two years before. A scramble-net can be seen furled-up along the ship's side.

these boxy-looking craft was – like so many other examples of Britain's rearmament programme – only built and tested a few months before the start of the war. The Admiralty ordered 18 in April 1939, with another eight in September on the outbreak of war, and another 30 in March 1940. Self-propelled by two Ford V8 engines, at 41 feet long, weighing 9 tons with an 18-inch draft and a crew of four, they were designed to be carried in standard ships' lifeboat davits and had the ability to carry 36 fully equipped men right the way up to a beach, allowing them to exit in seconds through the bow, which lowered to form a ramp. With careful handling to ensure the additional weight of men entering, rather than exiting, didn't leave them aground, they could also do the reverse far more efficiently than normal ships' boats, and their armour-plated mahogany hulls provided vastly greater protection to those inside. Eight of the 13 landing craft ultimately used off Dunkirk were lost and they were officially credited with bringing just 118 men back to Britain, but such figures only reflect the numbers offloaded directly from the vessel onto British soil. Along with all the other small vessels working the beaches, the numbers ferried by them, 50 at a time on innumerable trips from the beaches out to the bigger ships for the latter to take home,

Royal Marines charge from the bow of an assault landing craft of the type used at Bjerkvik and Dunkirk, during an exercise in 1941.

were never recorded, and in this they were invaluable.

The other, radical, solution was the involvement of the smallest, most numerous, most varied, and most famous type of vessel involved in the evacuation: the personal pleasure craft that would epitomise the little ships after the war. The vast majority were gathered up

The 56-foot river cruiser *New Britannic* brought 86 men back, alongside those ferried from the beaches to waiting ships. Retired in 1991, *New Britannic* has been restored and is in private ownership.

from the boatyards and ports of southern England and crewed primarily by officers and men from the Royal Navy's manning depot at Chatham.

The stories attached to them are as varied as the vessels themselves. Some, such as the 26-foot motor yacht

Chalmondesleigh (or Chumley), comedian Tommy Trinder's 26-foot motor yacht, still in private ownership.

The 52-foot motor yacht *Bluebird of Chelsea*, was requisitioned by the Admiralty in 1939, serving throughout the war, and is now in private hands.

The 73-foot motor yacht *Chico*, was also briefly owned by Sir Malcolm Campbell before the war and requisitioned by the Admiralty in 1939. *Chico* took part in the Calais operation before evacuating 317 men from Dunkirk, and has since been restored and is in private ownership.

Chalmondesleigh, were famous already. Built in the United States in 1934 and owned by the comedian Tommy Trinder who regularly made a play on the name of his boat a part of his act, Trinder's brother sailed *Chalmondesleigh* from the Isle of Wight to Shoreham to be taken over by a naval crew and sailed across the Channel. Surviving the Dunkirk experience and returned to Trinder at the end of the war, *Chalmondesleigh* passed through a number of private hands and underwent restorations (and a name shortening to *Chumley*), taking part in various commemorative events. Similarly, the 107-foot motor yacht *Bluebird*, built in 1938 and owned by the famed world speed record holder Sir Malcolm Campbell, was also present, along with two of his former yachts, *Chico* and the now *Bluebird of Chelsea*, all of which survived both the war and the peace, and can now be found in Rotterdam, Scotland and London, respectively.

Other vessels had rather more controversial owners, such as the 11-foot motor launch *Advance*, which – unusually

— was initially crewed by owner Colin Dick and his friend Eric Hamilton-Piercy, who were prominent members of Oswald Mosley's British Union of Fascists. Upon their return to Ramsgate both were detained for 90 days and *Advance* returned to the beaches skippered by Sub-Lieutenant P. Snow. The fate of *Advance* is unfortunately unknown.

Perhaps the most famous story among the pleasure craft, almost by proxy as much as by retelling, is that of the motor yacht *Sundowner*, which was owned by the remarkable Charles Lightoller. By the summer of 1940, Lightoller had already led an extraordinary life. A mariner from the age of 13, he was the most senior officer to survive the loss of the *Titanic* in 1912. During the First World War he helped pioneer aerial navigation over water aboard the Grand Fleet's seaplane carrier HMS *Campania* before being given command of three destroyers, sinking the U-boat *UB-110* in controversial circumstances while commanding the last of these, HMS *Garry*, in June 1918. Retiring from both merchant and

The 52-foot motor yacht *Wairakei II* was requisitioned by the Ministry of War Transport in 1939 and commanded by Lieutenant Leyland at Dunkirk. *Wairakei II* has since been restored and is in private ownership.

The 45-foot motor yacht *Gay Venture*, was built in 1938 for the former racing driver Douglas Briault. Yacht and owner found themselves in naval service after the outbreak of war, the former making Dunkirk, the latter being let down by Motor Launch 341 on the way to St Nazaire in 1942.

naval service after the war, the now Commander Lightoller bought and restored the former Admiralty pinnace *Sundowner* in 1929, and when the call came for Dunkirk, he gathered his eldest son Roger and a Sea Scout called Gerald Ashcroft, setting sail on 1 June, bringing 122 men back to Ramsgate. Although this was the beginning and end of Lightoller's second war, *Sundowner* continued in naval service as a coastal patrol

Sundowner, Charles Lightoller's motor yacht.

vessel until being returned to Lightoller in 1946. Helmed by Lightoller's by then 80-year-old widow, Sylvia, *Sundowner* took part in the Channel crossing by some of the pleasure vessels that had been organised by the television personality Raymond Baxter for the 25th anniversary of the evacuation in 1965. *Sundowner* later passed through a number of private owners and the East Kent Maritime Trust, before ending up in

The 50-foot motor yacht *White Marlin* was requisitioned by the Admiralty and attached to the HMS *Fervent* shore-base at Ramsgate. *Gay Venture* was Captain Tennant's personal transport at Dunkirk and was among the last to leave.

The 29-foot motor yacht *L'Orage* came to be at the heart of commemorating the evacuation at Dunkirk after being purchased by Raymond Baxter in 1963.

PREVIOUS
PAGES
Trimilia (behind
Wairakei II), was a
48-foot Ramsgate
Lifeboat, one of
just two RNLI-
crewed Lifeboats
at Dunkirk,
rescuing 17 men.
Finally retiring
as a lifeboat in
1953, *Trimilia* has
been restored as
a private yacht.

the hands of the Steam Museum Trust, who display the yacht at the Ramsgate Maritime Museum.

At the heart of the post-war story of the pleasure craft lies *L'Orage*. A 30-foot motor yacht built in 1938 and originally named *Surrey*, *L'Orage* was among the many small pleasure craft requisitioned from the boatyards and moorings along the Thames and dispatched to Dunkirk. Raymond Baxter bought the craft in 1963 and had it restored to its former glory, *L'Orage*'s history inspiring him to organise the 25th anniversary Channel crossing in 1965. With the subsequent creation of the Association of Dunkirk Little Ships, Baxter became the Honorary Admiral, with *L'Orage* as his flagship. Now in new hands, following Baxter's passing in 2009, *L'Orage* continues to participate in commemorative events.

Not every pleasure craft that survived both Dunkirk and the war has a happy history, however. Ownership of a historic vessel is often summed up as a constant battle with time and the elements that is neither easy nor cheap. Some simply fall into disrepair, decaying on river banks and at moorings, and in certain, dramatic cases, sinking there, as happened to the 40-foot motor cruiser *Compass Rose*, in the River Lark, near Isleham in Cambridgeshire; it had to be scrapped in March 2019. Others are touched by tragedy, such as the 85-foot Thames river cruiser *Marchioness*, which had an astonishingly long career starting in 1923, and resuming in 1945 after a wartime hiatus, ending on the night of 19–20 August 1989 in a catastrophic collision with another vessel that claimed the lives of 51 partygoers.

Thanks to the work of dedicated volunteers, and owners, and in some cases, funding, there is hope for some vessels that have fallen into hard times, such as the 50-foot motor cruiser *Skylark IX*. Having sunk in Loch Lomond in 2010, *Skylark IX* was rescued from the brink of destruction with aid from Britain's National Lottery in December 2018 – an effort that helps to ensure the surviving 'Little Ships of Dunkirk' have a future.

OTHER EVACUATIONS AND THE BIG SHIPS

OPERATION *DYNAMO* WAS very much the peak of a series of Allied evacuations that took place in the summer of 1940, but it was by no means the end of them, for even as *Shikari* was making that last exit from Dunkirk harbour, 1,000 miles to the north a group of six big troop ships and the repair ship HMS *Vindictive* were pulling into Harstad in Norway. The order to evacuate that country had in fact been issued two days before the order to evacuate Dunkirk, but it had been delayed due to Allied desire not to leave without achieving at least something towards their strategic aim there. Consequently, the day Belgium fell, the Allied navies landed a brigade of French and Norwegian troops onto the beaches at Narvik, to briefly re-take the town and damage the port's facilities, severing one of Germany's main supply routes for vital Swedish iron ore for seven months.

Codenamed Operation *Alphabet*, the evacuation of Norway was planned and executed predominantly by the magnificently monocled (and monikered) Admiral of the Fleet William Boyle, 12th Earl of Cork and Orrery, a retired Commander-in-Chief Home Fleet with a reputation for aggression. It was in many ways the antithesis of Operation *Dynamo*, for where *Dynamo* was an evacuation of necessity in the face of massive German assault, despite German occupation of much of the country, *Alphabet* was an evacuation with a degree of choice. Allied forces were in no danger of being trapped and destroyed, but with previously neutral Italy now

Admiral of the Fleet William Boyle, 12th Earl of Cork and Orrery.

The 20,175-ton Cunard liner RMS *Franconia* was requisitioned as a troopship, taking part in the evacuations of both Norway and of France a few days later, surviving the war having transported an estimated 189,239 troops around the world.

threatening the Mediterranean, and the situation across the Channel as it was, priorities simply told.

Another key difference was that where Operation *Dynamo* was and remains to this day defined, rightly or wrongly, by the 'little ships', Operation *Alphabet* was very much a 'big ship' operation. Cork needed to lift just 25,000 men out of Harstad, but had to transport them several hundred miles, and where much of the equipment in France was simply rendered inoperable and abandoned around Dunkirk, 'the troops, ships, guns and certain equipment are urgently required for the defences of the United Kingdom', read the orders. Anti-aircraft guns were a noted priority. The vessels used off Norway were therefore of a different order to those off Dunkirk. Just 26 ships were involved, but they were predominantly the likes of Cunard's big ocean liners *Georgic*, *Franconia*

and *Lancastria*, each displacing more than twice even *Clan Macalister*.

This extended to warships too, for Norway was the theatre of the great ships of the main fleets. Virtually the entire frontline strength of the Kriegsmarine, from battleships to U-boats, had been dedicated to the invasion in April and the British had responded with

the full might of the Home Fleet. It was a commitment that had continued throughout the campaign. Vice Admiral Lionel Wells' aircraft carrier squadron – HMS *Ark Royal*, HMS *Glorious* and HMS *Furious* – was particularly prominent. Though lacking in numbers and performance, their Skuas and Swordfish supplied much of the Allied air power in Norway, both for the fleet and forces ashore, including during the evacuation; most RAF fighters lacked the range to fly there and fight, and in any case were understandably committed to operations in the south.

Flying his flag aboard the battleship HMS *Rodney* at Scapa Flow, the Home Fleet's current commander-in-chief, Admiral of the Fleet Sir Charles Forbes, had to keep an eye on developments to the south too. Holland's Channel Force had been disbanded once the initial transport of the BEF had been completed in October 1939, so Forbes now needed to counter any moves against the evacuations in the Channel, or even the British coast itself. He did so with noticeably reduced resources, however. In April the increasing Italian threat had necessitated the reconstitution of a powerful Mediterranean Fleet, forcing a reduction to Forbes' hitherto overwhelming strength. Then, on the very final day of the evacuation at Dunkirk, Admiral Wilhelm Marschall sailed

HMS *Ark Royal* (with a Swordfish from 820 NAS), was the Royal Navy's most modern and powerful aircraft carrier in 1940, enjoying a brief but spectacular career that included the hunt for the German battleship *Bismarck*, before being sunk by the U-boat *U-81* off Gibraltar in November 1941.

Admiral of the Fleet Sir Charles Forbes, whose Home Fleet was perhaps the ultimate guardian of the evacuations.

The 41,250-ton battleship HMS *Rodney* was, with sister ship HMS *Nelson*, arguably the most powerful in the world in 1940, famously going on to help sink the German battleship *Bismarck*, and later to support the D-Day landings.

from Kiel with the battleships *Scharnhorst* and *Gneisenau*, the heavy cruiser *Hipper* and four destroyers. Emerging from the Skaggerak, they headed north.

This would appear a questionable choice given the destruction such a force could have wrought in the Channel at any point over the preceding week, particularly since the Germans were in fact unaware Operation *Alphabet* was happening. However, despite the terrifying vulnerability of the streams of ships and boats racing to and from France, the open waters off Norway always offered a far better tactical scenario for Germany's few, precious, big ships. The waters of the Channel were almost claustrophobically enclosed, with little room to manoeuvre, hide or escape, and filled with perils including Allied minefields, coastal forces and aircraft. Even the elderly *Courbet* and *Paris* at Cherbourg posed a threat with their big 12-inch guns. It would fall to the Luftwaffe and the Kriegsmarine's own coastal forces to try to stop Operation *Dynamo* and subsequent evacuations from France, while Marschall's fast, powerful force, was to try to help reverse the apparent Allied victory at Narvik.

GNEISENAU.

The 38,900-ton battleship *Gneisenau* was fast and well armoured but had relatively small guns. Nonetheless, along with sister ship *Scharnhorst*, *Gneisenau* was arguably the most successful of Germany's conventional battleships before being disabled in February 1942.

The aircraft carrier HMS *Glorious* and her sister ship *Courageous* were both lost in controversial circumstances in the first year of war.

Although the troop convoys and heavy cruiser HMS *Devonshire*, which was evacuating the Norwegian government and royal family, all made it back to Britain, Marschall did not miss the unexpected opportunity to inflict a spectacular and bloody defeat upon this Allied evacuation. On 8 June, his two battleships found and sank *Glorious* and the destroyers HMS *Ardent* and HMS *Acasta*, which had been controversially detached from Wells' aircraft carrier squadron. The two RAF squadrons that had been sent to Norway were also caught up in the disaster. Desperate to evacuate with their equipment too, 46 and 263 squadrons had remarkably managed to land their Hurricanes and Gloster Gladiators on *Glorious*' flight deck to make the journey home, only to be sunk with the ship. The loss of one of Britain's precious few big, fast aircraft carriers, two destroyers, two valuable fighter squadrons and 1,563 men was a significant blow and the biggest Royal Navy loss in a single incident during the entire war. Caught by surprise, Forbes began what became a series of hunts for Marschall's ships by air and sea.

On 13 June he caught them, launching an air strike from Wells' flagship, HMS *Ark Royal* as they lay in harbour at Trondheim. Eight weeks earlier the Skuas of 800 and 803 Naval Air Squadrons had bombed and sunk the light cruiser *Konigsberg* at Bergen, but this was a vastly different prospect. Lacking both the numbers and performance to overwhelm the defences, or bombs able to damage battleships, this time there was to be no spectacular victory. The Skuas suffered heavy losses, inflicting no damage.

Gneisenau sailed into Kiel on 28 July, the last of Marschall's three big ships to successfully make it back, drawing a line under the Norwegian campaign. Yet, while they had managed to escape 'sinking honourably' in a showdown with Forbes' main force, torpedoes from *Acasta* and Lieutenant Commander David Ingram's submarine HMS *Clyde*, ensured that neither battleship would sail again until the following year. The rest of the campaign had taken a savage toll on the Kriegsmarine too. One of its most powerful cruisers would not leave the yard for a full year. On top of this, another three cruisers and ten destroyers had been sunk – fully half the Germans' entire fleet of the latter type of ship. The Royal Navy's aircraft, destroyers and, particularly, its submarines, commanded by First World War submarine ace Vice Admiral Sir Max Horton, had performed remarkably. Before Norway there had been little enough chance of the Kriegsmarine's surface fleet being able to seriously contest the Channel, either to interfere with evacuations or to protect an invasion of Britain. After Norway, even that was essentially gone.

Despite the incredible success of Operation *Dynamo*, the day Dunkirk fell Britain still had over 140,000 men left in France, and although surplus, non-fighting men were still being withdrawn, the fight for that country was far from finished. The day after Dunkirk fell the Germans began the second stage of their invasion of France. Frequently overlooked compared with the events of May, this involved

von Rundstedt's Army Group A, again as the main thrust, pushing south across the River Aisne and round to the rear of the Maginot Line, with von Leeb's Army Group C once more attacking the line itself, while von Bock's Army Group B pushed west across the Somme and up the Channel coast.

Major General Victor Fortune (R) after surrendering the 51st Highland Division to Erwin Rommel (L), on 12 June 1940 at St Valery.

Determined to stem the tide, and bolstered by thousands of new troops, alongside those returning from Britain after their evacuation at Dunkirk, the French had reconstituted their Seventh and Tenth armies in a new defensive line named for their new Supreme Commander, General Maxime Weygand. They had learned much in the preceding weeks and, despite the name, Weygand had arranged his forces not in lines, but by transforming the local towns and villages into fortified redoubts nicknamed 'Weygand hedgehogs', with 360-degree defences, ordering them to hold out until relieved by Allied armour. Well dug in, supplied and motivated, the French were preparing to fight the sort of defensive battle they had long

Admiral Sir William James possessed a keen interest in naval history, publishing a number of books both during his time in uniform and after his retirement in 1942.

anticipated and trained for. For the Germans, this time there was to be no magic bullet of fast, manoeuvring panzers and air power, for unlike in May, crucially, Weygand's defences lay right across their lines of advance. They were now forced into direct and bloody assaults with infantry, leading to their worst casualties of the campaign in France. Meanwhile, in his famous speech the day the last ships left Dunkirk, Churchill had already announced the intention to rebuild the British Expeditionary Force, once more under Gort. The first elements of the 52nd Lowland Division began arriving at Cherbourg on 7 June, followed by the 1st Canadian Division at Brest on 12 June. Also arriving at Cherbourg that evening, in a small Dutch steamer, came their corps commander, the newly knighted Lieutenant General Sir Alan Brooke.

It would not be enough, however. German breakthroughs at Rouen on 9 June left the British needing to evacuate Le Havre. Ordered that day, Operation *Cycle* was organised by the Commander-in-Chief Portsmouth, the highly capable and intelligent Admiral Sir William James. Freshly reinforced by the Canadian HMCS *Restigouche* and HMCS *St Laurent*, James' destroyers and other vessels were able to carry 11,059 men out of the way of the German advance by 13 June, though weather and opposition ensured that they could not rescue much of the 51st Highland Division, trapped at nearby St Valery, which was forced to surrender on the 12th.

By the 14th it was becoming clear that the French Army was in a state of collapse, and following a meeting with Weygand, Brooke found himself involved in what was to become the first of many volcanic clashes between the Prime Minister and himself that would continue throughout the war. Churchill eventually conceded to an exhausted Brooke some half an hour later, authorising the final withdrawal of British forces from the continent of Europe. Once again, the first to leave would be elements of the RAF, the surviving bomber squadrons of the Advanced Air Striking Force flying back to Britain on 15 June, Barratt having had the same – albeit perhaps slightly less fraught – conversations with Air Chief Marshal Sir Cyril Newall and the Air Ministry.

Admiral Sir Martin Dunbar-Nasmith V.C. (left).

Codenamed Operation *Aerial*, the planning for the naval side of this evacuation was to fall upon James once more, and his opposite number as Commander-in-Chief Plymouth and

Admiralty House, the Commander-in-Chief Plymouth's residence, with headquarters tunnels beneath (now a private property).

The 25,579-ton battleship *Courbet* evacuated to Portsmouth after defending Cherbourg, being captured by the British on 3 July and handed to the Free French. *Courbet* was scuttled as a breakwater on D-Day.

Western Approaches, Admiral Sir Martin Dunbar-Nasmith, a legendary Victoria Cross-winning First World War submariner. Looking after the remaining Channel ports and the Channel Islands, James had the more immediate task. Even aided by *Courbet*'s immense firepower, the defences of Cherbourg could not hold forever, so with little or no rest from Operation *Cycle*, his ships set about their work, and by the afternoon of 18 June, the last of 30,630 men had been evacuated; 21,474 were brought away from St Malo. Both were surrendered after demolition of their port facilities. Meanwhile, another 25,000 were evacuated from the Channel Islands before their occupation on 30 June.

Responsible for evacuating the westernmost ports such as Brest, St Nazaire, Nantes and Bordeaux, Dunbar-Nasmith found himself with a different set of problems. Having to cover many more ports, further from home, over a wider area, that potentially contained many more men, Dunbar-Nasmith needed some serious shipping capacity. He received it in the form of the big ocean liners *Strathaird* and *Otranto*, as well as much of the group that had brought

Allied forces out of Norway just a week before. Scheduled for refit and leave after evacuating 2,653 troops from Harstad, *Lancastria*'s crew had instead been recalled and sent south, dropping anchor off St Nazaire early on the 17th. They were soon surrounded by an assortment of tugs, tenders and other small harbour craft crowded with troops and civilians all wanting to board. At 1545 that afternoon, tragedy struck. Junkers Ju 88s of the Kampfgeschwader 30 hit *Lancastria* three or four times, and in just 20 minutes the great liner was gone. The *Lancastria* Association lists 1,738 known victims, but if the crew's estimates of numbers packed aboard are even close to being correct, the figure may well exceed 4,000, making *Lancastria* Britain's worst ever maritime disaster. Caught in the aftermath was Brooke, evacuated to Plymouth aboard the trawler HMT *Cambridgeshire*, whose crew had been pulling survivors from the sea just hours before.

The following day in Bordeaux, one of the most crucial meetings of the war took place. Despite the approach of German forces, Admiral of the Fleet Sir Dudley Pound, First Sea Lord

SS *Nomadic*, the 1,273-ton tender to the ocean liners *Olympic* and *Titanic* had been renamed *Ingenieur Minard* by 1940, and evacuated troops from Cherbourg in 1940, before returning to France after the war and finally ending up at her birthplace as part of the Titanic Belfast museum.

The Cunard liner RMS *Lancastria* was requisitioned as a troopship, took part in the evacuations of both Norway and of France, but met a tragic end.

and professional head of the Royal Navy, had flown in, accompanied by the new First Lord of the Admiralty, Albert Alexander. They were there to meet Admiral of the Fleet François Darlan, their French counterpart as combined naval commander-in-chief and minister of Marine, to discuss the evacuation of the all-important French fleet.

Italy's declaration of war on 10 June added their significant fleet to what would soon become known as the Axis cause, hugely increasing Allied difficulties at sea, so the withdrawal of the French Navy at the conclusion of armistice negotiations would in any case be a major blow. However, if Germany took control of what was arguably the most powerful navy in Europe, and managed the tricky task of operating and sustaining even a significant fraction of its ships, Britain's position at sea would face a serious threat, despite the successes off Norway. Should fears about Japanese

Admirals Darlan and Pound, influential yet controversial figures who led their respective navies through the first years of war.

intentions in the Far East then be fulfilled, that position would become perilous in the extreme. On the other hand, if an agreement could be reached persuading Darlan to join the Polish and Dutch in allowing his fleet to continue the fight in exile alongside the Royal Navy, Pound and Alexander would pull off a truly spectacular coup. If not, then at least the fleet needed to be either secured and demilitarised in British or American ports, or, in extremis, scuttled. Time was frighteningly short, however. The brand new battleships *Richelieu* and *Jean Bart* – among the most powerful in the world – still lay at Brest and St Nazaire respectively, just hours from falling into German hands.

Darlan gave Pound and Alexander his word of honour (backed by an explicit order two days later) that the fleet would never fall into German hands. He also revealed that *Richelieu* had already sailed that morning, with *Jean Bart* following the next day, a remarkable feat for the crews as – much like half the Dutch ships the previous month – both were essentially still under construction and had never before been to sea. However, unlike the Dutch, or even *Courbet* and

The 47,548-ton battleship *Richelieu*, and sister ship *Jean Bart*, matched the speed, armour and firepower of the new *Bismarck* and *Littorio* classes of Germany and Italy. Handed to the Free French Navy in 1942, *Richelieu* spent the rest of the war with the British Home and Eastern Fleets.

Paris, they did not sail north for Portsmouth or Plymouth, but south for Dakar and Casablanca respectively, creating a powerful, modern, North Africa-based fleet alongside the new battlecruisers *Dunkerque* and *Strasbourg* at Mers-el-Kebir. Believing, as many others in the French government did, that Britain too would soon be forced to sue for peace, perhaps in as little as five weeks, Darlan chose to remain in France. His control of the fleet ensured his position as a key member of the new government of Marshal Philippe Pétain, victor of the Battle of Verdun and perhaps the last of France's great First World War generals, who had replaced Reynaud in the aftermath of Churchill's failed proposal for Anglo–French political union on 16 June.

Unsatisfactory though this may have been for the British, with the French Navy gone, scenes at Brest and St Nazaire on the 18th soon closely resembled those at Cherbourg. The convoy carrying away the last of 32,584 Allied personnel from Brest was followed by the demolition party aboard the destroyer HMS *Broke*, smoke rising behind them from the destruction they had wrought upon the facilities of France's most important naval base in the Atlantic.

With better port facilities than Dunkirk and more big ships, some equipment was also being evacuated in Operation *Aerial*, including some unusual and highly secret material. On the 19th Lew Kowarski and Hans Halban, two of France's most eminent nuclear scientists, joined the exodus at Bordeaux, boarding the cargo ship SS *Broompark*. They brought with them machine tools, industrial diamonds, their supply of deuterium oxide (otherwise known as 'heavy water', a vital ingredient in nuclear energy), and crucially, 33 of their colleagues, all of which would be incorporated into Britain's burgeoning nuclear weapons programme, the curiously codenamed 'Tube Alloys' project, which would merge with the famous 'Manhattan Project' in the United States two years later.

The BBC broadcast that day by the Polish Prime Minister and commander-in-chief, General Władysław Sikorski, echoing the one made by de Gaulle on the 18th that urged his countrymen to join him in continuing the fight from Britain, ensured that thousands of Polish troops would now need evacuating. This was made more difficult by the fact that that much of Operation *Aerial* had been concluded on the 18th, leaving many of the key ports in ruins, shipping having sailed and RAF air cover flown. The signing of the Franco–German Armistice on 22 June further complicated matters. Nonetheless, a large number of Poles made a remarkable retreat south to the port of St-Jean-de-Luz, near the border with Spain. Dunbar-Nasmith once more sent ships. Under the command of Rear Admiral Alban Curteis, the Polish liners *Batory* and *Sobieski* were supplemented by the likes of the troop transports *Arandora Star* and *Ettrick*, the cruisers HMS *Galatea* and HMS *Calcutta*, and destroyers HMS *Harvester*, HMCS *Fraser* and HMCS *Restigouche*. The weather proved to be a double-edged sword, hindering embarkation as well as any Luftwaffe attempts to interfere, but the evacuation proceeded and at 1530 on the 25th, fully three days after the armistice had been signed, the convoy sailed.

The Blue Star Line cruise ship SS *Arandora Star* served as a troopship in the evacuations of Norway and of France, but was sunk by a U-boat in July 1940.

Late that evening, *Fraser* tragically became the last ship to be lost during the evacuations after being accidentally rammed by *Calcutta*. Sixty-four lives were lost from both ships. It was Canada's first significant naval loss of the war. What was left of the Polish Army reached Britain on 27 June, finally joining the navy ten months after its evacuation from Gdynia under the Peking Plan.

Operation *Aerial* evacuated 191,870 troops of varying nationalities from France, including 144,171 British, 24,352 Poles, 18,246 French and 4,938 Czechs. The liner *Lancastria* was its only major loss. Taken together with the other evacuations, from a standing start, a multi-national fleet of vessels, ranging quite literally from rowing boats to ocean liners, had evacuated nearly 600,000 men from ports 1,000 miles apart across the continent of Europe in just 31 days. Perhaps unsurprisingly with operations extemporised at such short notice, not everything had gone as might have been hoped, while losses in defeat were grievous. The British Army lost 10,000 dead in France alone, with another 58,000 wounded and made prisoners of war. Equipment losses included some 65,000 vehicles, including around 450 tanks, and nearly 500,000 tons of stores, fuel and ammunition. The RAF and Royal Navy lost nearly 1,000 aircraft across the main campaigns, while approximately 200 Allied vessels, civilian and naval, great and small, had been sunk. Naval losses across the evacuations alone included an aircraft carrier, 11 British, three French and one Canadian destroyer, with two cruisers and another seven destroyers (including one French and one Polish) sunk in the general fighting round Norway. Worst of all, Belgium, Denmark, the Netherlands, Norway and even France itself had joined Poland and Czechoslovakia under German control, while Italy had opened another front in the Mediterranean.

The geography of the war had been utterly transformed, largely to Britain's detriment. With control of these countries came control of their air bases, which now played host to the Luftwaffe, and although they had yet to seriously respond to Britain's bomber offensive, with airfields now well within flying range, they would soon be testing that country as never before. The Battle of Britain would have to be fought and the Blitz endured. Meanwhile, that same bomber offensive now assumed vastly greater significance in Britain's military strategy as the most visible symbol of the country's capacity not just to continue to fight, but to take the fight to Germany.

This new geography affected not only the war in the air, but also the war at sea, for the Germans now occupied these countries' strategically vital ports too. Those on the Channel coast would soon begin filling with invasion barges. Those in Norway and on the French Atlantic coast almost immediately began filling with U-boats. The first arrived at Lorient on 5 July. Freed from the Norwegian campaign, Dönitz's U-boats returned to the Battle of the Atlantic with a vengeance, and with their new bases 800 miles further west than before, could now range deeper into the Atlantic for longer, without the need to fight or sneak their way past defences to the north and south of the British Isles. It would become known to the U-boat crews as the first 'happy time' (*Die Glückliche Zeit*). Merchant ship losses surged (though the addition of the large Dutch and Norwegian merchant fleets helped the Allied effort considerably). Meanwhile, Luftwaffe bombs and mines, alongside Kriegsmarine coastal forces in the Channel, would soon make the great southern and eastern ports such as Southampton and even London itself essentially untenable to all but coastal shipping. The big, transoceanic vessels would be forced to concentrate in the northern and western ports such as Liverpool and Glasgow, slashing Britain's capacity to import the materials that were the lifeblood of its people and its war effort, and causing enormous disruption to supply lines ashore.

By comparison of course, mere fractions of the armed forces of the former allies had managed to make the journey to join Britain to continue the fight, and the fate of the vital

French fleet remained uncertain. In the following weeks and months, the continuing tensions over this would result in the deaths of more than 1,000 French sailors at Oran and Dakar, and the former allies all but at war with each other. In one of the more startling of many examples of this reverse, the defences at Dakar were marshalled by none other than Rear Admiral Marcel Landriau, commander of Ramsay's French flotilla off Dunkirk just three months before. When the long-feared German attempt to capture it came, however, the French fleet kept Darlan's promise, scuttling itself at Toulon on 27 November 1942.

Despite everything, Britain with its vast empire remained a military and economic colossus, particularly in the air and maritime spheres, and German victories had not been cost-free either, particularly in those self-same spheres. Norway and other actions had all but shattered the Kriegsmarine's small surface fleet, while any amphibious fleet for a cross-Channel invasion attempt would similarly have to be largely improvised. The heavy losses of the opening months, and a low-priority building programme in an economy still suffering under British blockade and not yet fully geared for war, meant lack of U-boat numbers would be a key limiting factor in this new phase of the Battle of the Atlantic, despite the arrival of 26 Italian submarines at Bordeaux in August. Already short on training, doctrine and equipment for either maritime or strategic bombing campaigns, the Luftwaffe, too, had suffered significantly. Operations in Belgium, France and the Netherlands had cost 1,284 aircraft, Norway some 260 more, on top of another 280 or so in Poland. Alongside the bombers and fighters needed to fight for air superiority in the forthcoming Battle of Britain, around 300 Junkers Ju 52 transport aircraft vital for the airborne assaults of the Fallschirmjäger (among other things) had also been lost in Norway and the Netherlands. There would be dark days ahead, but Britain would not fall too.

THE FIVE-YEARLY
COMMEMORATIVE RETURNS

DUNKIRK WAS, IN the words of Churchill's famous speech the day the evacuation ended, 'A miracle of deliverance, achieved by valour, by perseverance, by perfect discipline, by faultless service, by resource, by skill, unconquerable fidelity…'. As he warned, it was by no means a victory. Indeed, the reality was one of catastrophic defeat that transformed the war at sea, on land, in the air and at home, but it was an epic deed that few would deny deserves a place in any pantheon of wartime feats.

One particular aspect of the story has captured and held the imagination like no other, and that, of course, is the participation of the little ships. The tale of the collection of private pleasure craft from across southern England and their use in the evacuation was cemented into the popular imagination early. The day after Churchill spoke, J.B. Priestley made his broadcast lauding the *Gracie Fields*, describing 'another English epic… so typical of us, so absurd and yet so grand and gallant that you hardly know whether to laugh or cry'. Priestley's 'English epic' was not about 'the warships, magnificent though they were', but instead 'the little pleasure steamers' and the clashing worlds of the peacetime English holiday resort and the horrors of contemporary war. This was followed later that year by Paul Gallico's bestselling short story, 'The Snow Goose', about a disabled sailor who joins the evacuation in his own boat. Then the multi-Oscar-winning 1942 Hollywood film *Mrs Miniver* portrayed the civilian, boat-

John Boynton 'J.B.' Priestley, whose broadcast on 5 June 1940 perhaps first framed popular perceptions of the evacuation of Dunkirk and the little ships.

owning husband of the titular heroine answering the call on 27 May, and sailing his motorboat *Starling* up the Thames, apparently joined by an ever-expanding flotilla of his fellow pleasure-boat skippers heading across the Channel to save the army from France in a tremendously evocative sequence. In 1958 the Ealing Studios film *Dunkirk* further emphasised this theme, with two of its central characters, Charles Foreman and John Holden (played by Bernard Lee and Richard Attenborough), being portrayed as private boat owners who join others in making the trip across the Channel.

The presence of Lightoller and others off the beaches of course demonstrates that this sort of action was not completely mythical, though the sheer preponderance of naval vessels and even naval crews aboard the civilian-owned 'little ships' themselves gives the reality a rather different shape to the one that has captured the imaginations of so many. Nonetheless this image of relatively ordinary civilians riding to the rescue of the army, against overwhelming odds, in their own small boats, so perfectly encapsulated and spoke to a particular set of national self-images – not just of a maritime nation of boat owners, but of a country fighting a 'people's war', united as one behind its armed forces to achieve incredible feats – that it endured and passed into legend. The continued hold of this image of the evacuation could be seen 77 years after the event, in the 2017 movie *Dunkirk*, where the actor Mark Rylance played Mr Dawson, a character directly inspired by the Lightoller story, who sails

Sundowner. Originally built as an Admiralty steam pinnace in 1912, and rescued from dereliction in the Medway by the Lightollers in 1929, the 58-foot motor yacht brought 122 men back from Dunkirk and is now kept at the Ramsgate Maritime Museum.

his boat, *Moonstone*, to the beaches, accompanied by his son and a young boy.

With the story of the little ships so central to the public image of one of the war's defining moments, it was perhaps inevitable that at some point efforts would be made to commemorate them. Perhaps key among these is the Association of Dunkirk Little Ships, which came into being in the aftermath of the 25th anniversary of the evacuation in 1965.

Central to it all was the television personality Raymond Baxter. Baxter joined the RAF after Dunkirk, but, having purchased *L'Orage*, he sent a letter to *The Sunday Times* in October 1964 declaring his intent to sail his vessel across the Channel for the forthcoming anniversary and asking other boat owners to join him. *The Sunday Times* at that point was edited by Denis Hamilton who, as a young, 21-year-old 2nd Lieutenant in the Durham Light Infantry, had stood awaiting rescue with his comrades from the beaches at Dunkirk. Hamilton readily published Baxter's letter and some 43 vessels joined him for the 25th anniversary crossing, together with the Royal Navy and the Royal National Lifeboat Institution. At a remarkable follow-up party that

Raymond Baxter joined the Royal Air Force as a fighter pilot in August 1940, joining the BBC after the war as a presenter and commentator. His purchase of the motor cruiser *L'Orage* was one of the key events leading to the creation of the Association of Dunkirk Little Ships.

December, the now Commander Charles Lamb approached Baxter and proposed the creation of an association of little ship owners. John Knight, who had participated in the anniversary crossing, then separately approached Baxter with the same idea, and the Association of Dunkirk Little Ships was born.

The association's foundation meeting was on 28 November 1966. Qualification for membership required current ownership of a proven Dunkirk Little Ship, defined as craft that took part in the evacuation in 1940 that were originally privately owned, though that has now been extended to former service vessels that are now in private hands, such as Wake-Walker's flagship MTB *102*. An association flag of the Cross of St George with the arms of Dunkirk was also created. Of what it estimates to be 400–500 surviving vessels in 2020, the association has a membership of over 150 vessels that took part in the evacuation in 1940. It meets at least three times a year, and little ships take part in events ranging from local regattas to royal jubilee celebrations. Several starred in the 2017 *Dunkirk* movie, including MTB *102*, *Princess Elizabeth* and *Papillon* (though 'Mr Dawson's' *Moonstone* was in fact *Revlis*, a 43-foot motor cruiser which, though built in 1939 in Rosneath, remained in Scotland during the evacuation). However, the main commemorative sailings across the Channel to Dunkirk itself take place every five years, with the Royal Navy and RNLI often providing an escort. It is always a tricky proposition that has to take into account weather

and navigating one of the world's busiest shipping lanes, co-ordinating a large group of mostly small boats of varying size and speed. Nonetheless, participant numbers average around 50 and perhaps the largest gathering was for the 60th anniversary in 2000, in which 62 little ships took part.

As the numbers of those who were there in that summer of 1940 sadly dwindle, the importance of physical, material links to give life and shape to those famous events for future generations will only grow. The Association of Dunkirk Little Ships and their vessels, of course, form a vital part of this, and fortunately, they are not alone. One of the most famous examples is Admiral Ramsay's headquarters at Dover Castle, which is now preserved as a museum, complete with a statue of Operation *Dynamo*'s commander. The Chatham Naval Barracks that supplied so many crews closed in 1984 to become university buildings. There is even more to be found at Dunkirk itself, along with the great memorial at the cemetery, maintained by the Commonwealth War Graves

Sundowner, Wairakei II, Bluebird of Chelsea and *Riis I* displaying the flag of the Association of Dunkirk Little Ships.

Statue of Admiral Ramsay looking out to sea at his former headquarters at Dover Castle.

Built in 1785, Bughtrig House in Scotland was Admiral Sir Bertram Ramsay's home. The house is still in the ownership of his family who are in the process of creating a museum dedicated to the admiral.

Commission. Next to the site of Vice Admiral Abrial's old headquarters at Bastion 32 near the East Mole lies the Dunkirk War Museum; the East Mole, too, still exists, and nearby one of its more noted visitors during the evacuation, the paddle steamer *Princess Elizabeth* lies moored, restored, now a floating restaurant. At Zuydcoote Beach (France) and others, the remains of shipwrecks such as the paddle steamers *Crested Eagle*, *Devonia* and the fabled *Gracie Fields* are still visible at low tide, some 80 years after the event, and it is possible to dive on some of the other shipwrecks further out to sea too. At Gdynia in Poland, the last surviving destroyer to have taken part, ORP *Błyskawica*, is now a museum ship.

Dowding's Fighter Command headquarters at Bentley Priory and 11 Group's at Uxbridge were both preserved too and

are, of course, as much Dunkirk museums as Battle of Britain museums. At least two Spitfires and a Hurricane that actually took part in the air battles above the evacuations survive. One of each is even airworthy, operating from the former RAF base at Duxford that is now run by the Imperial War Museum. Examples of other aircraft types that took part, including the Royal Navy's Swordfish, and the Luftwaffe's Messerschmitt Bf 109s, 110s, Junkers Ju 88s and Heinkel He 111s can be found,

Princess Elizabeth, now berthed in Dunkirk.

The Drill Hall of Chatham Naval Barracks, part of Admiral Drax's Nore command, which supplied much of the additional personnel and forces needed by Admiral Ramsay at Dover, particularly crews for the requisitioned Little Ships (now part of the University of Kent Medway campus).

though few, if any, of these were actually physically present. Similarly, just one example of the Kriegsmarine's E-boat torpedo boats that posed such a threat to the evacuations still exists. *S-130* is under restoration in Cornwall for the Leicestershire-based Wheatcroft Collection, though this particular example of the type was only built in 1943.

Of the other evacuations, though, there is considerably less evidence. A memorial to the terrible losses aboard the *Lancastria* sits at St Nazaire; another, to the sacrifice of the 51st Highland Division, at St Valery; and Calais has one too. The shipwrecks of the Norwegian campaign still litter the fjords, their dead commemorated at the great naval memorials at Devonport, Chatham, Portsmouth and Laboe. The remarkable ORP *Błyskawica* is once again perhaps the last significant warship to have survived from this campaign. Yet the headquarters of neither James nor Dunbar-Nasmith have been preserved, while SS *Nomadic*, former tender to the

HMS *Devonia*, another of Priestley's fabled 'little holiday steamers'. Requisitioned as a minesweeper in 1939, *Devonia* was beached at La Panne on 31 May following bomb damage.

The Plymouth Naval Memorial commemorates those lost aboard HMS *Glorious*, HMS *Ardent* and HMS *Acasta* during Operation *Alphabet*, among many others.

The memorial at Kallow Point Port St Mary, Isle of Man, incorporates an anchor salvaged from *Mona's Queen III*, sunk off Dunkirk on 29 May 1940. It is dedicated to those lost at Dunkirk from the Isle of Man Steam Packet Company and others in the Merchant Navy.

Dunkirk war cemetery and memorial, designed by Philip Hepworth, is run by the Commonwealth War Graves Commission.

The 60-foot yacht *Tahilla*, built in 1922 and named *Skylark* was among the vessels commandeered by the Ministry of War Transport and dispatched to Dunkirk. *Tahilla* returned to private ownership after the war.

Titanic and now preserved as a museum ship in dry dock in Belfast, is probably the last surviving ship of any size to have taken part in *Aerial*.

In truth, however, this is perhaps to be expected. Not everything can be preserved as a museum, so when the Ministry

The memorial to the sinking of the *Lancastria* on the former site of the William Beardmore & Sons shipyard on Clydebank where the ship was built.

of Defence sold Admiralty Houses at both Chatham and Plymouth, they were converted to university and residential buildings respectively; the great underground command posts from which Drax and Dunbar-Nasmith worked in 1940 were each stripped and sealed, though James's Admiralty House in Portsmouth remains a working part of that naval base. Equally, the bigger warships and passenger ships that participated in *Alphabet*, *Cycle* and *Aerial* (much like those that took part in *Dynamo*, of course), tended to be scrapped, rather than preserved, if they survived the war. Frequently objects of

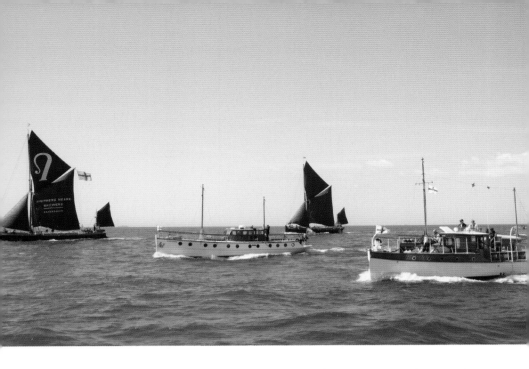

Greta, Sundowner, Pudgy and *Wairakei II* of the Association of Dunkirk Little Ships on their way across the Channel.

considerable affection from their owners and not subject to the imperatives of military or commercial obsolescence, the smaller, private yachts and river cruisers that took part in *Dynamo* in such numbers simply tend to fare better against the harsh realities of the economics of preservation than their larger brethren.

Yet the difference is not merely material. Remarkable as these other operations were in their own right, despite suffering their own, epic tragedies (including two of Britain's worst maritime disasters, just nine days apart, each with greater loss of life than the *Titanic* in 1912), despite even their intimate connections to *Dynamo* in effects, in timing, in ships involved, in people involved, Dunkirk and the little ships remain set apart in their iconic, and in some respects mythical, status. No great movies have been made about *Alphabet*, *Cycle* and *Aerial*, no equivalent statues to Ramsay's have ever been raised for their commanders – Cork, Dunbar-Nasmith or James – no phrase comparable to 'Dunkirk Spirit' has ever been coined about them, let alone entered the national lexicon. The sheer scale of that event, contained largely within a single, memorable, geographical point; the urgency and unexpected success of salvation in the very face of apparent enemy supremacy (at least on land, even if the story at sea and in the air

Tahilla and *White Marlin* of the Association of Dunkirk Little Ships, sailing alongside the East Mole at Dunkirk.

was rather different); the civilian participation in the form of the little ships: these and other unique features, woven together, mark out the story of Operation *Dynamo*, giving it its emotional resonance and power.

It is perhaps inevitable that time will soften even the profound cultural impact of Dunkirk and the little ships, as memories fade and those who were directly involved pass. However, their place as one of the defining stories of British involvement in an epochal war (and prelude to another of those defining stories in the Battle of Britain), is assured. At the same time, however, they form but one element – albeit the most memorable – in a momentous summer of evacuations that should never be forgotten.

PLACES TO VISIT

The Battle of Britain Bunker (11 Group's HQ), Wren
   Ave, Uxbridge UB10 0BE. Telephone: 01895 238154.
   Website: www.battleofbritainbunker.co.uk
Bentley Priory Museum, Mansion House Drive, Stanmore
   HA7 3FB. Telephone: 020 8950 5526.
   Website: www.bentleypriorymuseum.org.uk

Dover Castle, Castle Hill, Dover, Kent CT16 1HU.
Telephone: 0370 333 1181. Website: www.english-
heritage.org.uk/visit/places/dover-castle/things-to-do/
operation-dynamo-rescue-from-dunkirk

Dunkirk 1940, Magpie Hall Road, Chatham ME4 5ND.
Telephone: 01634 650839. Website: www.dunkirk1940.org

Dunkirk War Museum, rue des Chantiers de France,
Courtine du Bastion 32, 59140 Dunkerque.
Telephone: 333 28 66 79 21.
Website: www.dunkirk-tourism.com/What-to-see-do/
Dunkirk-1940/Dunkirk-war-museum

The Historic Dockyard Chatham, Main Gate Road, Chatham
ME4 4TZ. Telephone: 01634 823800.
Website: https://thedockyard.co.uk

IWM Duxford, Duxford, Cambridgeshire CB22 4QR.
Telephone: 02074 165000.
Website: www.iwm.org.uk/visits/iwm-duxford

Medway Queen, Gillingham Pier, Pier Approach Rd,
Gillingham, Kent ME7 1RX. Telephone: 01634 575717.
Website: www.medwayqueen.co.uk

SS *Nomadic*, Hamilton Dock, Queens Road, Belfast
BT3 9DT. Telephone: 02890 766386.
Website: www.nomadicbelfast.com

Princess Elizabeth, Quai de l'Estacade, 59140 Dunkerque,
France. Telephone: 33 7 82 63 99 09.
Website: www.princesselizabeth.eu

Ramsgate Maritime Museum (*Sundowner*), Clock House,
Pier Yard, Royal Harbour, Ramsgate, Kent CT11 8LS.
Telephone: 01843 570622.
Website: www.ramsgatemaritimemuseum.org

Ship Museum ORP "Błyskawica", al. Jana Pawła II 1,
81-345 Gdynia, Poland. Telephone: 058 620 13 8110.
Website: www.muzeummw.pl

The Association of Dunkirk Little Ships: www.adls.org.uk

INDEX

References to images are in **bold**.